ECONOMIC ANALYSIS AND PUBLIC ENTERPRISES

Optimal Pricing and Investment in Electricity Supply
(*a case study which supplements the present work*)

The Economics of Real Property
Interest Rates and Asset Prices
(*both out of print*)

ECONOMIC ANALYSIS AND PUBLIC ENTERPRISES

BY

RALPH TURVEY

Ex-Deputy Chairman of the National Board for Prices and Incomes
Sometime Chief Economist to the Electricity Council
Previously Reader in Economics at the London School of Economics

WITH A CONTRIBUTION BY
HERBERT CHRISTIE

ROWMAN AND LITTLEFIELD

TOTOWA, NEW JERSEY

First published in the United States 1971
by Rowman and Littlefield, Totowa, New Jersey

© *George Allen and Unwin Ltd.*, 1971

ISBN 0-87471-068-5

Printed in Great Britain

TO NICHOLAS AND AMANDA

PREFACE

On a number of occasions the National Board for Prices and Incomes, which has now been dissolved, had to examine the prices and efficiency of nationalized industries. Part of this work, though by no means all, related to optimal pricing and investment. In the first seven chapters of this book I have endeavoured to pull together some of the economic analysis of this subject which has proved useful. The remaining chapters consist of excerpts from Reports which applied this kind of analysis. They are included only as examples and do not pretend to be systematic or balanced accounts of any of the industries covered.

Herbert Christie drafted the last three chapters and I am mainly responsible for the rest. However all the Reports of the National Board for Prices and Incomes were the product of teamwork, so neither of us can claim all the credit for the six chapters reproduced from its reports. Nick Stevens and Maurice Shutler in particular both contributed a great deal to Chapter 10 on gas, as did Maurice Shutler in the case of Chapter 12 on coal.

Chapters 6 and 7 owe a lot to Steven Littlechild as I trust I have made clear in the text. Bill Baumol helped a great deal too, both by introducing me to Kuhn-Tucker analysis and by commenting on an early draft of the first part of the book. Michael Posner and Ivan Whitting also made helpful comments. I have an uneasy feeling that I may have forgotten some other kind critics, as the book has evolved over a fairly long period, starting as a course of lectures in economics held in 1969 at Lysebu near Oslo.

I am indebted to the Controller of Her Majesty's Stationery Office for permission to reproduce Chapters 8 to 13. Various omissions have been made and cross-references to other parts of the Report in question have been expunged or modified, but there are no changes of substance.

The book was completed by the end of January 1971, shortly before the National Board for Prices and Incomes was dissolved. On April 28, 1971, a Supplement to Report no. 153 appeared (Cmnd. 4455-I). This Supplement contains more material on the economics of the coal industry following on the two Appendices to Report 153 reprinted as Chapters 12 and 13 in this book.

London, June 1971

CONTENTS

1

INTRODUCTION

This book is about the economic efficiency of public enterprises; it deals with the analysis of costs, prices and investment. Economic efficiency is not all, of course; technical and managerial efficiency may be more important. The performance of an enterprise may, for example, depend much more on its labour relations than upon its pricing policy. But this book concentrates on economic analysis alone.

Some writers in the field aim for generality. Here, however, the criterion is usefulness rather than intellectual elegance. Instead of setting out some abstract formulation of optimal behaviour the aim is to provide some concepts and suggest lines of approach which are applicable in practice. Even where they cannot be applied quantitatively they may provide qualitative illumination which can aid decision-taking.

Consider as an example the standard theory of peak pricing as recently restated by Williamson.[1] In an elegant paper Mohring[2] has dispensed with some of Williamson's (and earlier writers') 'restrictive implicit assumptions', allowed for non-constant returns to scale and admitted certain constraints upon pricing. His analysis requires the existence of poll taxes to cover any deficit and to look after the distribution of income. At a more extreme level Kolm's recent book[3] endeavours to achieve such generality that it covers the provision of public goods as well as that of goods or services which are sold.

My approach, on the other hand, is to set out the principles one at a time as simply as possible. Their combination should only be

[1] 'Peak-load pricing', reprinted in Turvey, ed., *Public Enterprise* (Penguin, 1968).
[2] 'The Peak Load Problem with Increasing Returns and Pricing Constraints', *The American Economic Review*, Vol. LX, No. 4, September 1970.
[3] *Prix Publics Optimaux* (Editions du Centre National de la Recherche Scientifique, 1969).

attempted *ad hoc* to deal with the complications of a particular real case. Each real case will involve a different set of complications for two reasons. One is implicit above: the structure of production and marketing varies enormously from case to case. The other is more prosaic. It is that very often certain important parameters are unknown and can be estimated only very roughly. In such cases it is just not workmanlike to set up an elaborate model which requires that they be accurately known. It is surely better to succeed in moving in the right direction than to fail in an attempt to locate an unknowable optimum.

An example of the one-thing-at-a-time approach is to be found in Chapter 3. Parts of the analysis there depend upon and duplicate a paper written at my instigation by Rees.[4] His first-order condition for the *j*th good produced by the *i*th public enterprise turns out to be so complex that in order to explain it he has to take the expression one bit at a time. I have therefore preferred not to try to derive it all in one piece in the first place. My aim has been to minimize reader effort, which is not the same thing as either maximizing mathematical elegance or minimizing the number of pages.

For much the same reason I have refrained from adding knobs to the discussion of system costs in Chapter 6. I have in fact developed one elaboration of it with stochastic demand but since the result offered no additional illumination in abstract I have not included it here. Similarly I have omitted a Kuhn-Tucker analysis of the choice of generating plant and the cost structure in an electricity supply systems because it adds little to the more literary discussion of the matter in my *Optimal Pricing and Investment in Electricity Supply*.[5] In any case I have endeavoured to avoid duplication between that book and this. Although there is some overlap it should be regarded as a case study which supplements this book.

After all this (middle-aged?) contempt for elegant generality the reader will not be surprised if I omit any discussion of why public enterprises do or should exist. Nor shall I try to define what I mean by a public enterprise. Thus the problem of whether the approach is relevant to say, the Italian state monopoly of the import of bananas

[4] 'Second-Best Rules for Public Enterprise Pricing', *Economica* N.S., Vol. XXXV, No. 139, August 1968.
[5] (Allen and Unwin, MIT Press; 1968.) I have set out the algebra in *The Economic Journal*, no. 322, June 1971, pp. 371–5.

cannot be solved definitionally. Indeed one chapter tackles a problem which relates to what is definitely a private enterprise.

This book is about optimizing; about maximizing or minimizing something or other subject to this or that constraint. I do not propose to engage in textual exegesis of statutes to find out what, if anything, legislatures wanted public enterprises to do when they brought them into being. Nor shall I examine the fascinating question of what the objective functions of the leaders of public enterprises actually are. Instead the analysis is normative, and I choose to start with the resounding platitude that the aim of a public enterprise should be to maximize:

Social Benefit minus *Social Cost*

subject to any relevant constraints. By 'Social' I mean to society as a whole.

The next step is to make a series of strong assumptions, namely that:

1. The distribution of real income is not the concern of a public enterprise so that it should act as though that distribution were always ideal.
2. The customer is always right.
3. There are, unless specified, no externalities either of production or consumption.
4. What is not known should be ignored.

These assumptions taken together imply that the Social Benefit generated by a public enterprise is measured by its customers' willingness to pay for its outputs and that its money costs differ from its Social Costs only in respect of specified externalities and known divergences between the price of inputs and the value of their marginal products in other uses. The last assumption also justifies the use of partial equilibrium analysis.

Let it be clear that I do not personally believe that the first two assumptions are generally true. There are particular reasons for thinking otherwise in particular cases. Thus in tackling any particular problem it may be necessary to modify either assumption in a particular way. But as it is easiest to take one thing at a time, most of the following argument takes these assumptions for granted.

An example may help. The idea that other postal users should subsidize the transmission of reading matter for the blind is one that many people approve of. But in order to discuss optimal postage rates in general it seems best to start by ignoring the point to start with, bringing it in at the end as a modification of the conclusions. It is even more sensible to ignore it in putting forward elements of analysis which apply not merely to the postal services but to all sorts of public enterprise. By and large, therefore, the following chapters proceed *as if* Willingness to Pay did measure Social Benefit.

2

FINANCIAL PERFORMANCE OF
PUBLIC ENTERPRISE

Decisions about the prices and outputs of a public enterprise will result in a particular total revenue and total costs and a corresponding profit or loss. It has been usual in theoretical discussions of public-utility pricing to say that, when prices are equated to marginal costs, there will be a profit or loss according to whether the enterprise suffers increasing or decreasing costs with respect to scale. But this kind of argument is based on traditional textbook cost curves where the long-run cost curve shows the minimum costs attainable for each of a series of alternative output levels, assuming that a new industry is built from scratch, using today's technology and acquiring all inputs at today's factor prices. This is of no practical interest.

Whether or not marginal-cost pricing would produce a profit or loss in an orthodox accounting sense, on the other hand, depends on whether marginal costs exceed or fall short of average accounting costs. Since the latter reflect the technological and financial history of the industry as mirrored in its present state, no generalization is possible about the circumstances which will generate an accounting profit or loss. In any case, accounting profits or losses are only deemed to be of interest because, though arbitrary in measurement, people are used to them. They are the only kind of information normally available to the public, both for public and for private enterprises. Consequently it is natural to want to judge the former by the standards of the latter in terms of this information. It is thought reasonable that, apart from any use of a public enterprise as a vehicle for subsidizing particular groups of workers or consumers, a public enterprise should provide a rate of return on capital comparable with that earned by private enterprises. While the roughness of the yardstick is admitted, its defects are regarded as practical ones rather than ones of principle.

Efficient resource allocation, however, i.e. maximizing Total Social Benefits less Total Social Costs, is a matter of what is produced and how it is produced. Unfortunately, there is no relationship between the conditions for such maximization and accounting profits. It is, of course, true that an increase in efficiency will lower accounting costs. Otherwise, however, the accounting rate of return on total assets of a public enterprise means little. In particular it does *not* approximate the average of the d.c.f. rates of return on past investments and so does not indicate whether these past investments were, on average, reasonably successful.

This unwelcome conclusion has been rigorously demonstrated by Professor G. C. Harcourt. He proves that even under ideal conditions where 'uncertainty is absent, expectations are fulfilled, and the rate of profit has an unambiguous meaning' it is the case that 'as an indication of the realized rate of return the accountant's rate of profit is greatly influenced by irrelevant factors'. He concludes that anyone 'who compares rates of profit of different industries, or of the same industry in different countries, and draws inferences from their magnitude as to the relative profitability of investment in different uses or countries, does so at his own peril'.[1]

While accounting profits and the accounting rate of return are thus poor guides in themselves, they happen to be closely related to what is a significant magnitude, namely the net cash flow between a public enterprise and the Exchequer. Indeed it is probably a poorly articulated awareness of this which lies behind many people's intuitive belief that the accounting rate of return on total assets must somehow be of importance despite the logic of the arguments against it as a meaningful magnitude in its own right.

The net cash flow from a public enterprise to the Exchequer, which may be positive or negative, is made up as follows:

	Revenue
minus	*Accounting costs*
plus	*Depreciation*
plus	*Interest on government debt*
minus	*Capital expenditure*

Both revenue and costs depend, among other things, on the level of prices charged by the public enterprise. Hence the net cash flow partly depends upon these prices. Putting this the other way round,

---

[1] 'The accountant in a golden age', *Oxford Economic Papers* XVII (1965), reprinted in *Readings in the Concept and Measurement of Income*, ed. R. H. Parker and G. C. Harcourt.

if the size of the cash flow is something which matters to the Government, then the desired cash flow is one of the factors relevant to optimal price setting.

One way in which this point can be introduced formally is to modify the objective function by including in it some function of net cash flow. Thus if net cash flow is F the objective function can be rewritten as:

$$\text{Total Social Benefit} - \text{Total Social Cost} + f(F) \quad (1)$$

where df/dF is the 'marginal social value' as estimated by the Government of the net cash flow. If, once again, Total Social Benefit is assumed to be measured by willingness to pay and cost to the enterprise to represent Total Social Cost, this objective function becomes:

$$\text{Willingness to Pay} - \text{Cost} + f(F) \quad (2)$$

Alternatively, the Government may require F to be some given magnitude $\bar{F}$, so that the task of the public enterprise is to maximize Total Social Benefits less Costs subject to the constraint that $F = \bar{F}$. With the same assumptions as those just made this is equivalent to requiring maximization of:

$$\text{Willingness to Pay} - \text{Cost} + \lambda(F - \bar{F}) \quad (3)$$

where λ is the Lagrangian multiplier.

(2) and (3) are obviously closely related. In the former the marginal social value of F is preordained and the magnitude of F emerges. In the latter the magnitude of F is preordained and λ emerges as the marginal social net value. If F and $f(F)$ are set so that $df/dF = \lambda$ the two formulations give identical results.

In practice, governments find it easier to think in terms of a desired target $\bar{F}$ (without explicitly contemplating the value of its dual, λ) than to specify a function $f(F)$. This is not a matter of lack of Government sophistication in economic theory. F, after all, is part of the Government's budget and budgets do have to be set out in monetary terms. df/dF is implicitly positive because Government likes to be able to increase other expenditures or to lower taxes. All this has a general theoretical justification in terms of welfare economics, as recently explained by Baumol and Bradford.[2] Government

---

[2] 'Optimal Departures from Marginal Cost Pricing', *The American Economic Review*, Vol. LX, No. 3, June 1970. They ignore the contribution to the subject made by Serge Kolm in his *Prix Publics Optimaux*, which I personally found stimulating, albeit obscure.

clearly needs money and so must raise taxes. But taxes on other things inevitably make the prices of those other things different from their marginal costs. Hence the prices of the public enterprise's products must also differ from their marginal costs if resource misallocation is not to result. The cash flow requirement laid upon the public enterprise is equivalent to a set of taxes upon its products. To impose no such requirement would thus be equivalent to selling them tax-free in a world where many other things have to be taxed quite heavily. This would obviously result in resource misallocation. Hence the proposition that 'generally, prices which deviate in a systematic manner from marginal costs will be required for an optimal allocation of resources, even in the absence of externalities'.

The argument so far has been timeless so that investment by a public enterprise has not been mentioned. If we bring it into the picture, the formulation has to run in present worth terms and it becomes necessary to specify a rate of discount to be used in present worth calculations. If this is done, the principles of the analysis remain unchanged. There is an alternative formulation where Government lays down a pricing policy, a discount rate and a financial target. As these three requirements may not be mutually consistent, this formulation can be confusing, so we shall ignore it.

3

SECOND BEST

Much of the discussion of optimal pricing by public enterprises which is to be found in the literature is couched in terms of general equilibrium analysis. Despite its intellectual elegance this approach will not do here. We are concerned to derive rules for the behaviour of one, or a group of public enterprises which will maximize the Social Benefit of their activities less their Social Costs, given the environment within which they work, so the rules can only cover things under their control. Furthermore, if the rules are to be of any practical use they must not require the public enterprises to know things which it is in practice impossible for them to ascertain.

The analysis in this and subsequent chapters therefore has three features: it relates to second-best optimization, it is partial rather than general equilibrium and it is rough and ready. Thus the reader may notice occasions when, for example, bringing in the production function of a supplier would make possible an extension or more general formulation of the analysis. But such opportunities have been deliberately rejected on the grounds that public enterprises normally cannot get hard numerical information of this sort.

As explained in Chapter 1 it is assumed that market demand – willingness to pay – measures the social benefit of consumer goods, without committing the reader to agreeing that the income distribution is fair, that externalities in consumption are negligible and so on. Another expository simplification made to start with is that time is ignored. Thus this chapter and the next consist of elementary comparative statics of a fairly traditional sort. None the less they produce some quite useful answers; time is not the essence of *all* problems.

Since partial analysis is about a part of the economy, it is useful to start with a realistic example. If we choose the fuel sector as the example it can be described as in the adjacent diagram where each arrow represents a flow of goods and services or a whole set of such flows, such as different kinds of oil product. If the part of the economy concerned with fuel is described like this, which is only one of several possible ways, then the analysis might examine the optimal pricing policy of all three nationalized industries. This would be extremely complicated. Here, since the aim is to enunciate general

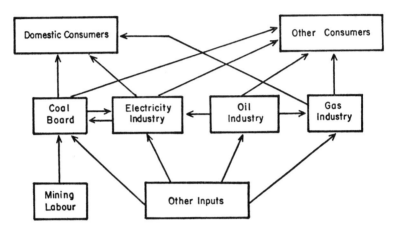

principles, it is best to tackle seriatim a few of the relationships involved in such a real case by means of simplified and stylized examples. These will now be constructed to consider demand interrelationships, the supply of an intermediate product to the producer of a final product, and the purchase of an intermediate product. Each of these cases will be considered separately and in turn.

The first relates solely to demand interrelations. A public enterprise produces a single product i in quantity x_i at a marginal cost of m_i which it sells to final consumers at a price of p_i. Various products j sold to final consumers by private enterprises are closely related in demand. The public and private enterprises alike buy the inputs which make up their marginal costs at prices which we take to represent the marginal social costs of each input. We assume this either because we know that this is the case or because we have no means of finding out whether or not it happens to be true. Thus the cost assumption is really that we have no good reason for supposing the price of any important input to diverge markedly in any particular direction from its marginal social cost and that we cannot even take the trouble to think about the question for the unimportant inputs. Even if, to take an extreme example, office carbon paper were bought from an avaricious monopolist, we would not bother about it.

In order to derive the marginal (first-order) conditions for optimizing p_i, the price charged to consumers by the public enterprise, we consider the effect of a small change in this price, Δp_i. This will affect not only the amount of i sold, x_i, but also the sales of the related goods, the x_j. The Social Benefit of this set of changes, which we are assuming to be the same as the willingness of consumers to pay for it, is measured in the case of all those related goods by:

$$\sum_{j \neq i} p_j \cdot \frac{\partial x_j}{\partial p_i} \cdot \Delta p_i$$

Each extra unit of j bought must be worth at least p_j to the buyer, for otherwise he would not have bought it, so this is a lower limit. Each unit of j dispensed with, in the cases where x_j falls, must have been worth no more than p_j, so in this case the expression is an upper limit. Thus the expression is only exact in the limit as Δp_i approaches zero.

For i itself, the good whose price changes, the consumers buying it before all valued an extra unit at less than p_i since they chose not to buy it, but valued the last unit bought at more, since they did buy it. A similar argument holds at the new price $p_i + \Delta p_i$. Thus the *average* value to consumers of each unit change in the amount of i bought is $p_i + \frac{1}{2}\Delta p_i$. This approximation is obviously rougher the larger is Δp_i and the greater the indivisibility of i. In an extreme case like houses or cars, where most consumers only have one or none, the approximation gets very crude.

Summing up, then, for all consumers' purchases of i and the j, the value to them of the change in their purchases, the Social Benefit of the change, is:

$$\left(p_i + \frac{\Delta p_i}{2}\right) \cdot \frac{\partial x_i}{\partial p_i} \cdot \Delta p_i + \sum_{j \neq i} p_j \cdot \frac{\partial x_j}{\partial p_i} \cdot \Delta p_i \qquad (1)$$

This result can also be derived from a utility-maximizing model of consumer behaviour, where it transpires that a constant marginal utility of income is required, i.e. that the income effect of Δp_i upon purchases of i and j must be zero. This is another way of saying that the degree of approximation involved is greater as consumers spend a larger proportion of their income on i and the higher is the absolute income elasticity of demand for i and the j.

The effect upon Social Costs of the output changes is simpler. The change in each output is just multiplied by its marginal cost m;

$$m_i \cdot \frac{\partial x_i}{\partial p_i} \cdot \Delta p_i + \sum_{j \neq i} m_j \cdot \frac{\partial x_j}{\partial p_i} \cdot \Delta p_i \qquad (2)$$

The net social gain being the excess of (1) over (2) we equate the difference between them to zero and get rid of Δp_i to get the marginal condition:

$$p_i \cdot \frac{\partial x_i}{\partial p_i} + \sum_{j \neq i} p_j \cdot \frac{\partial x_j}{\partial p_i} - m_i \cdot \frac{\partial x_i}{\partial p_i} - \sum_{j \neq i} m_j \cdot \frac{\partial x_j}{\partial p_i} = 0 \qquad (3)$$

This gives the optimal p_i as:

$$p_i = m_i - \sum_{j \neq i} \frac{\partial x_j}{\partial p_i} \cdot \frac{\partial p_i}{\partial x_i} \cdot (p_j - m_j) \qquad (4)$$

so that where the j are all substitutes for i, $\partial x_j / \partial p_i > 0$, p_i should exceed m_i if the p_j exceed their m_j, $(/)$ $\partial p_i / \partial x_i$ being < 0 $(/)$ and vice versa; conversely if they are all complements. If, however, some are the one and some are the other the application of the formula requires a good deal of information.

It will be noted that we have assumed that p_i must be the same for all consumers of i. Circumstances can be imagined, however, in which it might be better to differentiate between them. If, for example, some of the consumers of i also buy a complement but are not affected by the price of a substitute, while circumstances are the

24

opposite for another group of consumers, and if both the complement and the substitute are sold at well above marginal cost, then
Total Social Benefit less Cost would be maximized by charging the
first group $p_i < m_i$ and the second group $p_i > m_i$. This supposes, of
course, that the difference is not deemed unfair and that the arrange-
ment involves no extra costs, assumptions which may well not be
met in particular cases. The point is worth making all the same,
however, to show that once one is in the realm of second-best
optimization (sub-optimization), even the simplest conditions for
first-best (universal) optimization may sometimes cease to be relevant.

We now turn to our second simple type of market relationship.
Like the one just examined it is a type which is to be found in the
fuel sector. Here the box representing Other Inputs again relates to
ignorance rather than to knowledge, in the sense that we take their
prices to reflect their marginal social costs merely because we have no

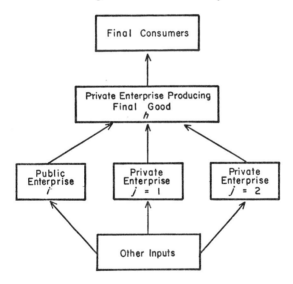

good reason for supposing otherwise. The relationship can be
shown diagrammatically as before. Here i, the product of the public
enterprise, is an intermediate good, sold to the producer of a consumption good h. The j are other intermediate goods used in the
production of h. We assume that the producer of h treats p_i and the
p_j as given, not exercising any monopsony power in respect of them.

Granted that the producer of h is free to decide how much i he buys, the value to him of a change in his purchase of it must be the resulting change in his profits. It thus equals the change in revenue less the change in the cost of other inputs:

$$\left(p_h + \frac{dp_h}{2}\right) \cdot dx_h + \left(x_h + \frac{dx_h}{2}\right) \cdot dp_h - \sum_j p_j \cdot dx_j$$

For any given p_i, profit maximization by the producer of h requires equality between the marginal cost to him of i, p_i, and the effect upon profits of a one unit change in his input of i:

$$p_i = \left(p_h + \frac{dp_h}{2}\right) \cdot dx_h + \left(x_h + \frac{dx_h}{2}\right) \cdot dp_h - \sum_j p_j \cdot dx_j \qquad (5)$$

where dx_h and dx_j represent the best way for him to use or save one extra unit of i. (We could, of course, formally derive these two magnitudes given a production function for h, but this is the sort of theoretical refinement which is not very helpful in practice.)

The elasticity of demand for h, E_h, is defined as:

$$E_h = \frac{\dfrac{dx_h}{x_h + \dfrac{dx_h}{2}}}{\dfrac{dp_h}{p_h + \dfrac{dp_h}{2}}} = \frac{\left(p_h + \dfrac{dp_h}{2}\right) \cdot dx_h}{\left(x_h + \dfrac{dx_h}{2}\right) \cdot dp_h}$$

so that:

$$\left(x_h + \frac{dx_h}{2}\right) \cdot dp_h = \frac{\left(p_h + \dfrac{dp_h}{2}\right) \cdot dx_h}{E_h} \qquad (6)$$

Substituting (6) into (5) then gives the profit maximizing condition for the producer of h as:

$$p_i = \left(p_h + \frac{dp_h}{2}\right) \cdot dx_h \cdot \left(1 + \frac{1}{E_h}\right) - \sum_j p_j \cdot dx_j \qquad (7)$$

This is now in a form in which it can be compared with the marginal condition for the use of i by the producer of h to be such as to maximize Total Social Benefit less Cost. If one more unit of i is produced at a marginal cost of m_i and is used by the producer of h, the resulting increase in the output of h will be worth $(p_h + dp_h/2) \cdot dx_h$ to consumers and the resulting change in inputs of the j will involve a Social Cost of $\Sigma m_j \cdot dx_j$. Hence the socially optimal marginal condition is:

$$m_i = \left(p_h + \frac{dp_h}{2} \right) \cdot dx_h - \sum_j m_j \cdot dx_j \tag{8}$$

Thus in order that what is most profitable for the producer of h (7) shall coincide with what is socially optimal (8), it is necessary, subtracting (8) from (7), that:

$$p_i - m_i = \left(p_h + \frac{dp_h}{2} \right) \cdot dx_h \cdot \frac{1}{E_h} - \sum_j (p_j - m_j) \cdot dx_j \tag{9}$$

which, transferring m_i to the right hand side and getting rid of dp_h gives the optimal p_i as:

$$p_i = m_i + \frac{p_h \cdot dx_h}{E_h} - \sum_j (p_j - m_j) \cdot dx_j \tag{10}$$

Since $E_h < 0$, the middle term on the right hand side tells us that, except when the elasticity of demand for h is infinite, i should be priced at below its marginal cost by an amount which is greater the less elastic is the demand (the greater is the monopoly element in p_h) and the larger is dx_h, i.e. the more the output of h is altered to use or save an extra unit of i.

The final term on the right hand side justifies an excess of p_i over m_i when substitute inputs to i are priced at above their marginal costs, $p_j > m_j$ and $dx_j < 0$. But if complementary j are priced at above their marginal costs then this, taken by itself, justifies pricing i at less than its marginal cost. We see, therefore, that with the relations shown in the last diagram, second-best optimal pricing of an intermediate good requires the public enterprise to pay heed to divergences of price from marginal cost both on the part of the customer firms who use its product as inputs and on the part of the suppliers of other inputs to those customers.

The difficulty of implementing this approach in such cases as electricity and railway transport, which are sold as intermediate products to thousands and thousands of customers, needs no emphasis. However, the size of the term dx_h is an important factor. This term is large enough to matter in the case of electricity used for smelting, for example, but small enough to forget, at the opposite extreme, in the case of office lighting as an industrial input. Furthermore, the analysis does not tell us that, to continue the example, monopoly in smelting *ought* to be dealt with by electricity pricing policy; it merely shows what factors would be relevant *if* the electricity industry were animated solely by the aim of maximizing Social Benefit minus Social Costs, *if* these were measured simply by willingness to pay and the cost of 'Other Inputs' respectively and *if* the inviolability of monopoly were accepted. None of these conditions is fulfilled in practice, so I am not committing the absurdity of deriving a practical policy conclusion from one little piece of analysis.

The third simple type of market relationship to be considered is shown in the adjacent diagram. If the input j used by the public enterprise is sold at above marginal cost the optimal behaviour of the

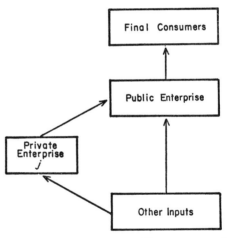

public enterprise is obviously to act as if p_j were equal to m_j. Once again, taken by itself, this would be an odd conclusion if it were regarded as a complete policy recommendation, since it appears as an open invitation to the producer of j to exploit the public enterprise! But the relationships to be examined will rarely be as simple as this. Any real case will involve some combination of the three simple cases just analysed as does, for example, the simplified description of the fuel section in the first diagram. Divergences between prices and marginal costs, which play a role in all these cases, may be due to factors other than monopoly. One is taxation and the other is external economies. The presence of the latter has so far been assumed away, but it is clear that in some cases a divergence between marginal social and private costs will involve a divergence between price and marginal social costs whose implications can be treated along the lines of the above analysis.

We can now sum up as far as we have got. The rules for maximizing Social Benefit less Cost in the absence of any constraints, and where final consumers' willingness to pay measures Social Benefit, boil down to the following: Look for large divergences between the prices and marginal (social) costs of the main inputs, items which are important complements or substitutes with the outputs and items for which the outputs constitute major inputs. If the pattern of such divergences is immutable, set prices of the outputs above or below their marginal costs according to whether the net effect of all these divergences is estimated (guessed) to make sales greater or less than they would be in the absence of the divergences. To act thus, in a manner inspired by the theory, is very rough and ready. So, however, is business life; the slopes of demand curves, the magnitude of cross effects and the marginal costs of other, private enterprises are rarely measurable in practice by even the most numerate advisers of a public enterprise.

Until now, the discussion in this chapter of the conditions for maximizing Benefits less Costs has assumed that there are no constraints upon maximization. As argued in Chapter 2, however, there are good reasons for imposing a cash flow target. We now bring this into the analysis, removing all the other complications discussed above. Thus the problem is to maximize:

$$Willingness\ to\ Pay - Costs$$

subject to:

$$Revenue - Costs = \bar{F}$$

Since this chapter is comparative statics, depreciation, interest and capital expenditure are ignored (or treated as constants) so that changes in costs are the same as changes in gross cash outflow.

The Lagrangian to be maximized is thus:

$$Willingness\ to\ Pay - Costs + \lambda(Revenue - Costs - \bar{F}) \qquad (11)$$

Maximization of this requires that its derivative with respect to the output of the ith product is zero, i.e.

$$p_i \quad - \quad m_i \quad + \lambda \left(\quad r_i \quad + \quad \sum_j \frac{\partial p_j}{\partial x_i} \cdot x_j - \quad m_i \quad \right) = 0 \quad (12)$$

$$\text{price} - \underset{\text{cost}}{\text{marginal}} + \lambda \left(\underset{\text{revenue}}{\text{marginal}} + \underset{\substack{\text{revenue} \\ \text{from other} \\ \text{products} \\ j}}{\text{effect on}} - \underset{\text{cost}}{\text{marginal}} \right) = 0$$

This formula includes both p_i the price, and r_i the marginal revenue of i which are related to each other and to the own-price elasticity of demand for i, E_i, by:

$$r_i = p_i + \frac{p_i}{E_i}$$

Using this, (12) can be manipulated to give the optimal price for i as:

$$p_i = \frac{m_i - \frac{\lambda}{1+\lambda} \cdot \sum_j \frac{\partial p_j}{\partial x_i} \cdot x_j}{1 + \frac{\lambda}{(1+\lambda) E_i}} \quad (13)$$

This tells us that the optimal price exceeds marginal cost, m_i, (E_i being negative) unless the other products j, are predominantly complementary to i. But assuming them mostly to be substitutes, the excess $p_i - m_i$ will be greater the more stringent is the constraint $\bar{F}$, the more important are the substitutes j and the lower is the own-price elasticity of demand for i. The stringency of $\bar{F}$ has an obvious effect. The importance of substitutes produced by the public enterprise arises because if they are many and close, a rise in p_i increases the revenue they provide more than if they are not. A low elasticity of demand, finally, means that a rise in p_i directly generates a lot of cash without much affecting output.

If cross-effects with other products are ignored, the ratio of price to marginal cost is simply greater the lower is the own-elasticity of demand. Thus relative outputs are not changed by the presence of the financial constraint. This is one of several ways in which the optimality conditions can be formulated.[1]

---

[1] See the papers by Baumol and Bradford and by Rees cited earlier which refer to relevant earlier writings by Manne, Boiteux *et al.*

λ, it will be recalled, is the gain in *Benefit* less *Cost* that would arise if the constraint $\bar{F}$ were reduced by one unit. This emerges clearly by re-arranging (12) to give:

$$\lambda = \frac{p_i - m_i}{m_i - \left(r_i + \sum_j \frac{\partial p_j}{\partial x_i} \cdot x_j \right)} \tag{14}$$

$$= \frac{\text{Gain in benefit less costs from unit increase in } x_i}{\text{Reduction in net cash flow from unit increase in } x_i}$$

Thus if the reduction in the net cash flow from a unit output increase is 50p, a £1 relaxation in the financial constraint will allow an increase in output of two units. If the excess of p_i over m_i is 20p the gain in Benefit less Cost, λ, will consequently be 40p. At the margin the government then implicitly values an extra £1 net cash flow from the public enterprise equally with a gain of 40p in Benefits less Costs. Since the £1 is a transfer, willingness to make this sacrifice to obtain it can be interpreted as a tacit judgement that the marginal excess burden of taxation is, or ought to be, 40 per cent.

4

SIMPLE VERSUS COMPLEX
PRICE STRUCTURES

It was pointed out in the last chapter in connection with one of the cases, that under certain circumstances optimization might require different prices to be charged to different customers for outputs produced at the same marginal costs. This, however, was subject to such price differentials not costing too much to administer and to their being publicly acceptable. By the same token, price differences which do correspond to cost differences may be too costly or unacceptable as, for example, in the case of charging different postage for letters between London and Birmingham on the one hand and Penzance and Inverness on the other.

In a case like this it is clear that if there is to be one uniform price it must, in the absence of any factors which make desirable a general difference between price and marginal cost of the sort so far discussed, be set at some sort of average of the relevant marginal costs. We now enquire how this average is to be calculated.[1]

Let the price which the ith customer is willing to pay as a function of the amount produced for him by the public enterprise, x_i be:

$$p_i = p_i(x_i)$$

The integral of this function is then his total willingness to pay. Summing over all consumers, assuming that they number n, then gives total Social Benefit as:

$$\sum_{i=1}^{n} \int^{x_i} p_i(x_i) dx_i$$

Social Cost, on the other hand, is a function of all the outputs:

$$C(x_1 \ldots, x_n)$$

[1] The following discussion of uniform pricing was stimulated by Coase, 'The Economics of Uniform Pricing', *Manchester School*, 1947.

The aim is thus to maximize:

$$\sum_{i=1}^{n} \int^{x_i} p_i(x_i)dx_i - C(x_1, \ldots, x_n) \tag{1}$$

subject to all the p_i being the uniform p. Writing m_i as before for marginal cost, the optimal p is found by differentiating (1) with respect to p:

$$p \cdot \frac{dx_1}{dp_1} + \ldots + p \cdot \frac{dx_n}{dp_n} - m_1 \cdot \frac{dx_1}{dp_1} - \ldots - m_n \cdot \frac{dx_n}{dp_n}$$

which, set equal to zero, gives:

$$p = \frac{m_1 \cdot \dfrac{dx_1}{dp_1} + \ldots + m_n \cdot \dfrac{dx_n}{dp_n}}{\dfrac{dx_1}{dp_1} + \ldots + \dfrac{dx_n}{dp_n}} \tag{2}$$

Thus the uniform p is obtained by weighting the marginal cost of each customer by the inverse of the absolute value of the slope of his demand curve. It is the absolute sensitivity of demand to price for each output which counts, not the size of each customer's demand. If outputs are sold to 1,000 customers for whom an alternative is available and to another 1,000 who have no access to a substitute, the price should be nearer the marginal costs of supplying the first group than those of the second.

This argument, since it rests upon the assumption that there are n consumers, relates to circumstances where there is an obligation on the public enterprise to supply all potential customers. Where such an obligation does not exist but where nevertheless only one uniform price can be charged, the choice of the optimal price is linked with the choice of which consumers are to be supplied. If the potential customers excluded from supply are those whose marginal cost is highest, their exclusion will lower the price charged to those who remain to a level equal to the weighted average of their marginal costs. This necessarily raises the Social Benefits of their consumption more than it adds to costs. The case for excluding the other consumers therefore merely requires that their willingness to pay (which we are still assuming to be the sole measure of Benefit) does not exceed the cost saved by not supplying them by more than this gain to the remaining consumers. If it falls short of the cost saving, than *a fortiori* they should be excluded.

The trouble with this kind of condition is that it requires knowledge of the excluded consumers' total willingness to pay rather than just their marginal willingness as measured by price. (It also requires knowledge of the total cost of supplying them as well as marginal costs, but the public enterprise can be expected to know both.) An algebraic formulation of the determination of the optimal area of supply would therefore not be very helpful. In practice the problem is often avoided, for instance by making a political decision to extend rural electrification to most of a country without any calculation of Benefit and Costs.

Just as the assumption that all potential consumers have to be served may require examination, so may the assumption that there has to be one uniform price. The impossibility of n different prices merely means, taken by itself, that there must be fewer than n prices, not that there must be only one.

Once again, the issue can be looked at in principle in terms of the effects upon Social Costs and Benefits of the alternatives available. A simple constructed example will serve to illustrate this.[2] It relates to rural and urban consumers whose weighted average marginal costs and total demand curves are denoted by r and u subscripts respectively. The choice lies between charging $p_r = m_r$ and $p_u = m_u$ on the one hand and:

$$p = \frac{m_r \cdot \dfrac{dx_r}{dp_r} + m_u \cdot \dfrac{dx_u}{dp_u}}{\dfrac{dx_r}{dp_r} + \dfrac{dx_u}{dp_u}}$$

on the other hand. Then if C represents the additional cost of charging two prices instead of one, there will be an increase in Social Benefit less Costs from shifting over from one price to two if:

$$\underbrace{(p_r - p) \cdot \frac{dx_r}{dp_r} \cdot \left(\frac{p + p_r}{2} - m_r\right)}_{\substack{\text{change in} \\ \text{rural} \\ \text{consumption}}} + \underbrace{(p_u - p) \cdot \frac{dx_u}{dp_u} \cdot \left(\frac{p + p_u}{2} - m_u\right)}_{\substack{\text{change in} \\ \text{urban} \\ \text{consumption}}} - C > 0 \tag{3}$$

[2] A diagrammatic version of this example is to be found on p. 97 of my *Optimal Pricing and Investment in Electricity Supply*.

$(p+p_r)/2$ here represents the average value to rural consumers per unit change in their consumption, and similarly with urban consumers. (Each unit of the fall in rural consumption is worth less to consumers than it costs while each unit of the rise in urban consumption is worth more.) Since p, p_r and p_u are all given in terms of m_r and m_u, this condition can be restated in terms of m_r, m_u, dx_u/dp_u, dx_r/dp_r, and C, but the resulting reformulation adds nothing to intuitive understanding of the issue so it is not given here. The main point is simply that both of the first two terms in (3) are positive, confirming the principle that it is only when C is positive that one price can ever be preferable to two.

While the choice between a simple and a more complicated price structure is illuminated by these principles it must not be supposed either that the costs and benefits can always be quantified in practice or that they encompass all relevant considerations. It may therefore be helpful to examine some particular problems where there is a choice between more complicated tariffs which reflect the structure of marginal costs relatively well and less complicated tariffs which do not.

Perhaps the simplest tariff of any public enterprise is the water rate levied upon domestic consumers. This involves no measurement of water consumption at all, but simply spreads out the share of the water undertaking's accounting costs borne by them according to the rateable values of their dwellings. As a cheap way of raising revenue, this pricing system can have few rivals. However it makes the marginal cost of water to the existing domestic consumer equal to zero and the total cost in respect of each new dwelling equal to some sort of average accounting cost.

Let us suppose it to be established that if all domestic users were to be charged marginal cost for their water by the introduction of metering there would be a net gain – apart from the cost of installing the meters. This assumed gain would involve a saving in the costs to the undertaking of avoiding or deferring the expansion of supply capacity. It would also involve a loss of benefit on the part of existing consumers from reduced consumption and, on the part of others, from occupying new dwellings elsewhere rather than in this supply area where, we assume, marginal cost is particularly high.

Under certain circumstances, it is conceivable that the gain would exceed the costs of universal metering. What particular conditions would have to be fulfilled for this to be the case does not matter here; the point to be made is that it would be wrong to focus attention solely on the choice between the existing system and such universal metering. There are at least two other possibilities.

Since the installation of meters in existing dwellings would be very expensive, one possibility would be to continue the existing system in their case and to introduce metering only in all dwellings built from now on. The benefits and costs would now depend only upon any resulting reduction in the rate of growth of new consumption, but the reduction in gain could be outweighed by a greater reduction in the cost of metering.

Suppose, again merely for the sake of argument, that this is likely and that the reduction in the rate of growth is expected to result from a reduction in the number of new dwellings constructed rather than from diminished consumption per new dwelling. Then much the same result could be achieved yet more cheaply by dispensing with the meters altogether and charging the occupants of the new dwellings both the same water rate as the existing consumers and, in addition, a 'connection charge' representing the capitalized excess of the marginal cost of supplying water to a typical dwelling over the water rate.

Whether or not this idea is relevant in British conditions, it serves to show two things. Firstly, a rough and ready reflection of marginal costs where demand is most elastic may sometimes be preferable both to reflecting them universally and to not reflecting them at all. Secondly, notions of fairness may play a crucial part – in this case the different treatment of existing and new consumers might well constitute a political objection even if the argument were otherwise well founded.

These two points also arise in the case of gas tariffs. So far as small consumers are concerned, these are all some function of quarterly consumption measured in therms. A quarterly charge plus so much per therm is common. This fails to reflect the structure of marginal costs particularly well. Let us assume (without at the moment examining the validity of the case) that either a higher price per therm in winter than in the rest of the year or the partial substitution of an additional charge proportioned to the consumer's gas take at peak periods would be preferable.

The trouble is that, possibly in contrast with the case of electricity, time-of-year or maximum-demand metering is prohibitively expensive in the case of small consumers. Hence, as in the case of water, it is appropriate to ask whether there is not some cheaper, albeit cruder, alternative to the existing system.

The roughest approximation to a price per therm which is higher in winter than at other times is a price which is higher for consumption billed for the winter quarter. But since, with quarterly billing, the meter-reading cycle is spread over three months, billings at the high price relating to meter readings made during December, January and February would cover periods ranging from three months ending in December for some consumers to three months ending in February for others. This would be inefficient, in that many consumers would not know when there was a price incentive for them to economize, and would also be regarded as unfair since different amounts would be paid by consumers with identical patterns of consumption. Furthermore, consumers due for a meter reading in the early part of the period would have an incentive to be out when the meter-reader called.

The first two objections would lose some of their force if the frequency of meter reading and billing were increased, but this would add considerably to costs.

An alternative which would avoid this drawback and provide a closer, though still imperfect approximation to the (postulated) ideal would be to charge each consumer a price per therm equal to a weighted average of the winter and the regular price, with the weights equal to the proportions of the period since the last meter reading falling within and outside the designated winter period. A clear message could then be given to all consumers that the price was higher in the designated period.

Turning now to the other idea, that of introducing some way of charging consumers according to their contribution to the peak without incurring the expense of maximum demand metering, there is a system applied by the West Midlands Gas Board to some large consumers which could also be used for domestic consumers. It, like the first idea, was set out in the NBPI second report on gas prices and was explained as follows:[3]

'It involves levying a charge proportional to the sum of the rated output capacities of a consumer's appliances, each appliance being multiplied by the average diversity factor for that type of appliance

[3] Gas Prices (Second Report), *NBPI Report No. 102* (HMSO Cmnd. 3942, 1969), para. 74.

according to its use by itself or in combination with others. The diversity factor (the ratio of appliance consumption at the time of system peak to its own maximum) is ascertainable and, indeed, already partly known as a result of market research. Appliance ownership, on the other hand, automatically becomes known on the occasion of conversion to natural gas. The only problem, therefore, would be to keep the record up to date. So far as appliance disposals are concerned, it would be in the interest of consumers to notify the Area Board. Acquisitions, on the other hand, could be checked in several ways: for example, by compulsory notification of appliance sales, compulsory inspection of new installation work (desirable in any case for safety reasons) or even inspection by meter readers. The creation and maintenance of the necessary records and their integration into the billing system would, of course, have a cost. The question is whether this cost would not be worth incurring. Any improvement in tariff structure will have a cost and the imperfect reflection of costs under the present system is such that some new tariff structure seems to us to be necessary. Furthermore, the records would have great value in forecasting; indeed, some boards are already thinking about the desirability of keeping consumer appliance records solely for this reason.'

In principle, the desirability of introducing one or other of these tariffs to replace existing domestic tariffs can be judged in terms of a calculus of benefits and costs along similar lines to those set out above. This obviously requires knowledge of consumers' reactions and the only feasible way of getting this knowledge is by experiment – a recommendation made to the United Kingdom gas industry by the NBPI but not so far accepted.

The British electricity industry is currently conducting an experiment of this nature. In this case more sophisticated metering is possible, for the obvious reason that electrical devices can be used, so the experimental tariffs all involve special meters unlike either of the two possibilities described above for gas.

The standard domestic tariff in all twelve Area Boards is either a simple two-part (fixed charge plus running rate) or a two- or three-block tariff. Off-peak restricted supply is available as an option. Boards currently offer a night and day tariff as an alternative, and the working of this tariff will be studied in parallel with the experiment. The three tariffs which are the subject of the experiment are:

Simple versus Complex Price Structures

1. A load/rate tariff, with disconnection of the over-load kilowatt-hour dial during night hours available as an option for an extra annual payment.
2. A seasonal tariff with a high kilowatt-hour rate for the three winter months and a low rate for the rest of the year. This involves a two-dial meter and a date switch. Existing off-peak restricted supply continues to be available as an option.
3. A seasonal time-of-day tariff with a high kilowatt-hour rate for the peak hours on winter weekdays, a low night rate and an intermediate rate for the remaining hours of the year. This involves a three-dial meter and a time switch. Since the night rate is similar to the rate for off-peak restricted supply, the latter is not available.

The rates are set so that for the average consumer in the experiment with an average time pattern or load the total bill would be the same as under the standard tariff. Two sets of rates are being applied under each tariff, each tariff sample being split into two sub-samples, in order to investigate the effect of different relativities within the tariff. Where the standard tariffs differ between Area Boards or are changed, the rates in the experimental tariff differ or will be changed correspondingly.

Consumers' adjustments to the experimental tariffs may involve change not only in the way they use their electrical appliances but also the acquisition of new ones and the disposal of existing ones. This means, on the one hand, that their adjustments will be gradual and extend over several years and, on the other hand, that their adjustments will be complete only if they regard their new tariffs as fairly permanent. Consequently the experiment will last five years (it started in winter 1966–7), but consumers have the right to continue for another five years if they wish. In addition, extension for a further five years will be granted if an appliance purchase hinges upon it, and if a consumer has the tariff suspended against his wishes within the fifteen years he will be compensated for expenditure undertaken specifically to benefit from the tariff.

The consumers in the experiment have been given a small initial payment and will receive a small annual payment so long as the experiment continues. This is to ensure that they are unlikely to lose and to compensate them for any inconvenience. The amounts are small enough to have a negligible income effect but, coupled with the interest of the experiment, sufficed to secure that over 85 per cent of consumers asked agreed to participate.

The number of consumers co-operating is 840 for each of the three tariffs. In addition there is a control group of some 900 consumers with matched characteristics on standard tariffs – a number which may be increased later on. Each tariff is operated in four geographically dispersed Area Boards, the consumers being selected from a primary random sample which was stratified to exclude all those with an annual electricity consumption more than a little below the national average and to give a greater weight to those with a high annual consumption. The reason for this is the *a priori* presumption that the extra cost of more complicated metering is not worth incurring for small consumers.

The information gathered includes household and dwelling characteristics, appliance ownership, acquisitions and disposals, and meter readings. In addition, for several months in each year, the consumption of one-third of each group is being recorded half-hourly using magnetic tape demand recorders which have been developed for load research by the industry. It is, of course, the information to be gathered in the fifth year which will be of most interest, and it is unlikely that any conclusions will be drawn until after 1972.[4]

While, in the case of electricity, technical progress makes possible more complicated price structures than could be contemplated some years ago, there are other cases where economic developments necessitate simpler structures. High density urban bus services furnish one example. Crew labour costs constitute about half of total costs with two-man operation, so the incentive to shift over to one-man operation is a considerable one and is one which increases as economic progress raises real wages. A recent estimate[5] suggests that with a 20–22½ per cent premium rate for one-man drivers plus a 50p per week bonus, the withdrawal of conductors from all services might reduce crew labour costs by about 28 per cent.

If, however, there continues to be a stage system of graduated fares and if drivers take over the collection of fares from the displaced conductors, these savings may be more than offset. The basic

---

[4] The last six paragraphs are taken from my paper, 'Peak-Load Pricing', *Journal of Political Economy*, Vol. 76, No. 1, January/February 1968.

[5] F. Fishwick, 'One-Man Operation in Municipal Transport', *Institute of Transport Journal*, Vol. 33, No. 9, March 1970.

reason emerges from the following table given by Fishwick. It relates to Luton:

BUS LOADING TIME IN SECONDS WITH MANUAL COLLEC-
TION OF GRADUATED FARES

No. of passengers boarding	One-man	Two-man
2	16	7
5	35	10
10	68	17
15	87	23
20	108	29
25	127	35

This shows clearly that bus overall journey speeds will decline with the introduction of one-man services so that more buses will be required to maintain frequency and passenger capacity in peak hours. The resulting cost increases can easily offset the savings mentioned above. Hence they have to be avoided by measures which increase passenger loading speeds. This requires a simplification of fare scales.

One possibility is to reduce the number of different fares so that the driver can issue fares more rapidly, less change-giving being required and fewer queries having to be answered. Fishwick quotes an example where a reduction in the number of fare values from nine to four reduced mean boarding time per passenger from 6·5 to 4·6 seconds.

The other possibility is to aid or replace the driver's function of issuing tickets by the use of turnstiles (as on London's Red Arrow buses), self-service ticket machines, or cash-fare boxes. The first two of these can give average loading times in peak periods of 2·5 seconds, but all three necessitate a flat fare or at least a coarsened fare structure.

Thus the introduction of one-man operation on high-density urban routes is only worth while if the fare structure is simplified. This can involve various problems as set out at length by Fishwick in his admirable paper. It will suffice here to mention only those arising with a flat-fare turnstile system. This has the advantage of eliminating fare evasion and a need for ticket inspection. On the other hand if the flat fare is not so high as to choke off many short-distance passengers it will either give long-distance passengers a very cheap ride or necessitate a new structure of circuitous routes so that long-distance passengers have to change several times. Unless tokens are used, fare-level changes to cope with inflation are confined to available coin values. Finally, old people, the disabled and people with baggage find turnstiles inconvenient. These are all quite important matters and may well render impossible the complete supersession of two-man buses.

5

QUALITY

The discussion so far relates to the pricing of one or more products of given quality produced by a public enterprise. Quality itself is a variable, however, which raises additional questions.

Consider first the case of a product produced at only one quality level. An improvement in this level will add both to costs and to willingness to pay. The effect on costs is readily calculable, but the effect on willingness to pay is not. Whereas the benefit of an extra unit of quantity is simply measured by the price for which the product is currently being sold, an extra 'unit of quality' raises the price which existing consumers will be willing to pay for the quantity currently being sold. Thus optimization, in the assumed absence of second-best complications, requires equality of the marginal cost of quality with the *sum* of the increases in willingness to pay for all consumers. This sum is obviously not observable and is difficult to estimate by market research. Thus the optimal condition, though easily stated, is not very helpful.

This lack of helpfulness and a possible solution can be illustrated by the example of a bus service. Here one aspect of the quality of output provided is the frequency of the service. Buses being indivisible units, it is obvious that outside peak hours there are usually some empty seats on each bus. This means that the marginal cost of taking an extra passenger at these times (the marginal cost of quantity) is zero. On the other hand, an increase in the frequency of service would necessitate the running of more buses, so that the marginal cost of quality is positive.

Even in principle, let alone in practice, the task of jointly fixing an optimal off-peak fare level and service frequency thus seems difficult. An answer may be sought by arguing that the aim should be to maximize Social Benefit less Social Cost, subject to the requirement that the users of the service pay in fares at least the Social Costs of providing it. If this is accepted, and if we simplify by thinking of a service between only two points, then the aim is to maximize

$$\sum_i W_i(n_i, f) - C(f) + \lambda\left(p \cdot \sum_i n_i - C(f)\right)$$

Here $W_i(n_i, f)$ is the willingness to pay of the ith passenger as a function of the number of journeys he undertakes and of the frequency of the service – the quantity and quality variables. $C(f)$ is costs as a function of frequency, the number of passengers being *ex hypothesi* irrelevant. p represents the price (fare) so that the last term is λ times revenue less costs.

The first-order conditions for this constrained maximization can now be obtained by differentiating the above expression with respect to quantity $\sum\limits_i n_i$, and quality f, and setting the resulting expressions equal to zero.

Since the partial derivative of total willingness to pay with respect to quantity is simply price p, we have, for the first condition:

$$p + \lambda\left(\frac{\partial p}{\partial \sum\limits_i n_i} \cdot \sum_i n_i + p\right) = 0$$

the term in brackets being the marginal revenue of quantity.

The second condition is:

$$\sum_i \frac{\partial p_i}{\partial f} - \frac{dC}{df} + \lambda\left(p \cdot \sum_i \frac{\partial n_i}{\partial f} - \frac{dC}{df}\right) = 0$$

Here the term in brackets is the effect on revenue less costs of a change in frequency.

Combining the two conditions gives:

$$\frac{p}{\dfrac{\partial p}{\partial \sum\limits_i n_i} \cdot \sum\limits_i n_i + p} = \frac{\sum\limits_i \dfrac{\partial p_i}{\partial f} - \dfrac{dC}{df}}{p \cdot \sum\limits_i \dfrac{\partial n_i}{\partial f} - \dfrac{dC}{df}}$$

i.e.

$$\frac{\textit{Gain in Benefit less Cost from}}{\textit{Marginal revenue of quantity}} = \frac{\textit{Gain in Benefit less Cost from}}{\textit{Marginal revenue of frequency}}$$
one extra passenger / increase in frequency; Marginal revenue of quantity (*no extra cost*) / Marginal revenue of frequency *less marginal cost of frequency*

44

The marginal cost of frequency can obviously be estimated and the marginal revenues of passengers and of frequency may be guessed at on the basis of experience. They are forecasts of what could be observed if frequency or fare were changed experimentally. But no amount of feasible experiment could give any clue as to the magnitude of

$$\sum_i \frac{\partial p_i}{\partial f}.$$

It is possible, however, to think in terms of a synthetic measure of the gain to passengers from an increase in frequency. This may be rough, but a rough measure is better than none. Frequency has to be determined anyway, so the difficulty of the problem does not mean that it can be avoided.

The least unsatisfactory approach to an answer starts from the obvious point that the gain to existing passengers from an increase in frequency is a reduction in average waiting time. This, and hence the total reduction in waiting time can be estimated. If the latter is then multiplied by an average value of passenger waiting time, we have a substitute for

$$\sum_i \frac{\partial p_i}{\partial f}.$$

Time saved or lost may be an aspect of quality change in the output of other public enterprises as well as those concerned with transport, so that this approach to the quality problem can be applied elsewhere. One example is telephone service, where congestion in peak periods leads to lost calls, giving 'line engaged' signals even when the telephone of the party being called is not engaged. Thus the appropriate price to charge for peak-period phone calls is related to the quality of peak-period telephone service and this can be measured by the delays involved in establishing calls. Once again, we can furnish a rough synthetic measure of subscribers' valuation of changes in the quality of service if a guess as to the value to them of saving a minute of delay can be made, a suggestion I owe to Professor Pyatt.

There is, of course, a purely technical relation between the number of phone calls and the quality of service. The telephone system is a large network of connected elements: lines and switching facilities. If A uses this system to call B he employs a subset of these elements to establish a connection and then to maintain it for the duration of the call. The capacity of the whole system is a matter of the total number of calls that can be made simultaneously. This is obviously a very complicated concept in a looped network and we shall not even attempt to define it. But clearly it is some function of the capacities of the individual elements, and something can be said about the capacity of each such element.

Consider, as an example, the capacity of a multi-circuit cable linking two exchanges. The traffic it carries is measured in erlangs, and an erlang is defined as:

$$\frac{Average\ duration\ of\ calls}{Average\ interval\ between\ start\ of\ calls}$$

which is the average number of calls being carried at any point of time. The theoretical (maximum conceivable) capacity of one circuit is thus one erlang; at the most it can carry ten six-minute calls or sixty one-minute calls per hour. But this could happen only if each call arrived just when the previous one finished. This does not happen; duration and interval are both stochastic. Hence queuing theory must be applied as it was by Erlang, a Dane, to ascertain the quality of service (defined as the probability of losing a call) as a function of the volume of traffic (measured in erlangs) and of capacity (the number of circuits).

As an example, if traffic is twelve erlangs then a twenty-circuit cable is required to give a ·01 probability of failure but if traffic is only two erlangs a six-circuit cable is required. The probability of failure is very sensitive to changes in capacity relative to traffic. Thus if, with the twenty-circuit cable, traffic falls from twelve to ten erlangs, the probability of losing a call falls from 1 in 100 to 1 in 500.

Similar relationships hold for other elements of the network and the quality of service of a series of elements roughly approximates to the sum of their individual qualities of service. Consequently the sort of relationship given in the example holds for the network as a whole. Thus for any given capacity, alternative combinations of quantity and quality are possible.

A good example of a different case of congestion is provided by a paper by Lester B. Lave and Joseph S. DeSalvo[1] on canal locks. Tows, each consisting of a towboat and a number of barges, arrive

---

[1] 'Congestion Tolls and the Economic Capacity of a Waterway', by Lester B. Lave and Joseph S. DeSalvo, *Journal of Political Economy*, Vol. 76, No. 3, May/June 1968.

at a lock at random intervals and have to wait to be locked through if the lock is being used when they arrive. The time then taken for locking through – service time – is also random.

Let the annual number of tows traversing the lock be K, so that the average hourly arrival rate is $K/8,760$; it is assumed that this rate is Poisson distributed. Let average service time be one hour; it is assumed that this too is Poisson distributed. Then queuing theory gives mean waiting-plus-service time as:

$$\frac{1}{1 - \dfrac{K}{8,760}}$$

Total annual waiting and service time is therefore:

$$\frac{K}{1 - \dfrac{K}{8,760}} = \frac{8,760\,K}{8,760 - K}$$

and the derivative of this with respect to K, the marginal social time cost of an extra tow per year, is:

$$\left(\frac{8,760}{8,760 - K}\right)^2$$

The marginal private time cost to an individual tow is simply its waiting and locking time. Thus the excess of marginal social over private time cost is:

$$E = \left(\frac{8,760}{8,760 - K}\right)^2 - \frac{1}{1 - \dfrac{K}{8,760}}$$

certain values of which are:

K	E
1,000	·15
2,000	·39
3,000	·79
4,000	1·55
5,000	3·10
6,000	6·93
7,000	19·82
8,000	121·19

If *V* is the hourly cost of keeping a tow waiting, then the optimal toll is *EV*, plus any avoidable operating costs of lock operation.

A third example of congestion is furnished in a paper on delays at airports by A. Carlin and R. E. Park.[2] At busy airports the sort of steady-state queuing model used above is not appropriate. Aircraft movement-rates approach mean service-time which, in a steady-state model, gives delays approaching infinity. But the aircraft movement rates fluctuate diurnally, so that the queue begins to be dissipated once the movement rate falls off. Consequently a simple deterministic queuing model is appropriate where each additional movement (arrival or departure) pushes back all subsequent movements until the end of the busy period by the service-time of the additional movement in question. Thus the marginal delay-cost of an additional movement occurring during a busy period depends on the number of movements during the remainder of the busy period and upon the costs per minute of delay for each of these movements.

Estimates presented by Carlin and Park for La Guardia Airport in New York in 1967–8 give marginal delay costs for the arrival of a large plane varying from zero in the small hours to just over $1,000 in the afternoon. Charges then depended only on weight (as they do at most airports) but in August 1968 the minimum charge, which is that paid by most small private aircraft (General Aviation), was raised from $5 to $25 between 8.00 and 10.00 hrs and 15.00 and 20.00 hrs on weekdays. Carlin and Park say that 'This pioneering but limited step in the direction of marginal congestion cost pricing, appears to have reduced significantly the amount of general aviation traffic at La Guardia.'

The three examples just discussed all involve time-costs which can sometimes be directly measured or indirectly inferred. Where quality is a matter of reliability, however, and is in joint supply to all customers, putting a value upon it may be impossible, in which case there is no alternative but to set some arbitrary standard to be met. Thus the extra value which domestic consumers of electricity would place upon a decreased probability of failure of supply has not yet been convincingly quantified. The difficulties involved can be readily seen by considering the kind of research which would have to be undertaken in order to provide an answer. It would involve knocking at

---

[2] 'Marginal Cost Pricing of Airport Runway Capacity', *The American Economic Review*, Vol. LX, No. 3, June 1970.

people's doors and saying 'Give me £1 or I will cut off your electricity'
Then either the money would be taken or the threat carried out! The
same procedure would be used for other sub-samples who would be
asked for other sums of money. Given a proper sampling design,
determination and total indifference to customer relations, an estimate of the demand for reliability could thus be constructed!

In some ways the choice of optimal quality by a public enterprise
is simpler when the product can be produced and sold in more than
one quality. This is not always feasible; there is, for example, little
possibility of providing some telephone subscribers with a more
reliable service than other subscribers connected to the same
exchange.[3] But where it is possible, consumers' free choices between
quality levels available at different prices can furnish information
which is not available when only one quality is sold. This information
is not sufficient, however, to feed into a formal analysis of the determination of the optimal set of price–quality combinations in order to
derive an empirical answer. The reason is that an analysis of this
sort postulates knowledge of what demands would be with each of a
large number of alternative such combinations. But in practice
public enterprises are already producing certain combinations, so the
practical question is merely whether they can be improved. If, for
example, two qualities are currently being produced and the sales of
the better one are rising relatively to the sales of the inferior one, this
fact is enough to suggest that an improved quality of either or both or,
alternatively, the introduction of a third and still better quality is
worth considering. Market research and, if it is feasible, trial marketing can then help to illuminate the decision which has to be
taken.

The most obvious examples of public enterprises providing mul-
tiple qualities of service are in the field of rail and air transport
where first-class is more spacious than other travel. Load-factor is
frequently lower in first class too, in which case the greater availability of seats at short notice is an additional factor making for
superior quality.

It is easy to suppose that the corresponding cost differences are
small so that the customary price excess for first-class travel, frequently of the order of 50 per cent, involves monopolistic price
discrimination. This may well be true in some cases, but the cost

---

[3] Though in Denmark operator-connected 'express' trunk calls are available
at double the normal rate for operator-connected trunk calls.

difference can be surprisingly large. Thus in an airliner, first-class places occupy about 50 per cent more space than other places and the proportion of airline costs which are related to aircraft flights rather than to the number of passengers carried is so large that, for the big jets, the cost ratio is about 1·4.[4]

Another example where customers are offered a price-quality choice is the French postal distinction between a 'letter' and a 'non-urgent' service and the British distinction between 'first-class' and 'second-class' service which has superseded the old distinction between letters and printed matter. In fact the nature of postal operations is such that it would be extraordinarily expensive not to have some differentiation of service and the new element is that all customers can now choose the quality of service whereas previously only those sending printed matter had the option of sending at either rate.

The basic reason why an equally expeditious handling of all mail would be very costly lies in the time dimension of postal operations. These involve three natural peaks during the twenty-four-hour cycle. First, over half of the letters received for outward sorting arrive between 16.00 and 19.00 hrs and those which are to be delivered in distant places on the following day have to be dispatched in time to catch evening trains. Second, in the case of mail which undergoes an intermediate sorting (at distribution offices) there is a peak which occurs around 24.00 hrs. Finally there is the early morning peak of inward sorting at delivery offices, followed by the morning delivery. It would be extremely expensive to provide an equivalent time-pattern of labour availability as this would involve awkward hours and split shifts (which are much disliked) for a majority of the postal workers.

This necessity is reduced somewhat though not, of course entirely avoided, by putting aside second-class mail in the evening (after facing and stamping) for sorting on the subsequent day. Most of this mail can then be delivered on the second day after posting, though some of it may be further deferred at the delivery office for second delivery or for third-day delivery. This latter possibility arises particularly at weekends, a complication which, together with variations in the size of mail flows between different pairs of points, means that the whole system is a great deal more complex than this

[4] Mahlon R. Straszheim, *The International Airline Industry* (The Brookings Institution, 1969), p. 101.

account might suggest. None the less, the major point is clear: labour costs are reduced by reducing the peak flow of work; this involves some deferment of some mail at certain points and the choice as to which mail shall be deferred is left in the hands of the customers of the Post Office in the light of their needs and of the differential in postage rates. The inferiority of the second-class service consists both of a longer average time from posting to delivery and in a greater variability.

While, as explained, formal analysis of optimal quality levels would not be a useful exercise, it is worth while saying a little about the problem of whether or not to introduce a new product of a given degree of superiority over existing ones. Suppose that each of the existing qualities $e = 1 \ldots n-1$ is currently sold at a price p_e equal to its existing marginal cost m_e. Now let the new product be introduced and sold at p_n in a quantity:

$$x_n = \sum_{e=1}^{n-1} T_e + N_n \tag{1}$$

T_e being demand transferred to n from e and N_n being new demand. The remaining demand is satisfied at the new set of p'_e reflecting the new set of m'_e, the prime distinguishing these from the old set.

The gain to a consumer from shifting from one of the e to purchasing a unit of the new quality must equal or exceed $p_n - p'_e$ while the value to completely new consumers must exceed p_n; otherwise neither would buy any of n. Hence the willingness to pay for x_n equals:

$$\sum_{e=1}^{n-1} T_e \cdot (p_n - p'_e) + p_n \cdot N_n + U$$

where U is the total (unknown) excess. The effect on costs, on the other hand, will be

$$C_n - \sum_{e=1}^{n-1} T_e \cdot \left(\frac{m_e + m'_e}{2} \right)$$

where C_n is the total cost of producing x_n and the term in brackets is the average saving over the range of output change from producing one less unit of e. Thus the effect on Total Benefit less Costs is:

$$\sum_{e=1}^{n-1} T_e \cdot (p_n - p'_e) + p_n \cdot N_n + U - C_n + \sum_{e=1}^{n-1} T_e \cdot \left(\frac{m_e + m'_e}{2} \right)$$

51

which, substituting from (1) and putting m'_e for p'_e, gives as the condition for introducing n:

$$x_n \cdot p_n + U + \sum_{e=1}^{n-1} T_e \cdot \frac{m_e - m'_e}{2} > C_n \qquad (2)$$

Since the second and third terms on the left-hand side are both positive (unless the e have falling marginal costs), equation (2) will be more than satisfied if:

$$x_n \cdot p_n \geqslant C_n$$

In other words: prospective revenue not less than costs is a sufficient condition for the introduction of the new quality unless existing qualities have falling marginal costs. The important feature of this result is that the loss of revenue from reduced sales of the e does not enter the picture as it would if profit maximization were the aim. If, therefore, the introduction of a new quality will, taken by itself, break even, it is certainly worth producing.

The discussion of quality in this chapter has proceeded as if there were no problem in distinguishing higher from lower quality. This is, of course, not generally true, but happens to be so in the case of many public enterprises. More frequent bus services, faster postal delivery, more comfortable railway carriages, fewer interruptions of electricity supply are all unambiguous quality improvements. Similar arguments apply to quality innovations which appeal only to some consumers, such as greetings telegrams. However there are other innovations which may appeal only if they are advertised and promoted, as was electric storage heating. Such innovations may be extremely valuable but unfortunately there is no coherent economic analysis of advertising available which can be used to examine the optimal advertising policy of public enterprises. Once we drop the assumption that consumers know what is good for them without being told about it, it becomes impossible to set out rigorous optimality conditions.

6

THE ANALYSIS OF MARGINAL COSTS

Previous chapters have ignored time and this chapter now introduces it. We now take account of the fact that outputs and inputs have a time dimension, that they must be dated. We have to think in terms of time-streams of inputs and outputs, of benefits and costs. This brings in investment, i.e. capital expenditure; and expectations about the future, which involve uncertainty.

It is tempting to try to deal with the implications of these complications for optimal pricing in terms of great generality. But three important practical considerations justify a simpler approach.

The first is that all decisions are not made now. We do not have to decide this year what to do next year; we only have to decide what to do this year. Next year and subsequent years are relevant now only because what it will be possible or desirable for us to do then will depend partly on what we have done this year. These future consequences of present actions can only be ascertained, however, by making hypothetical future decisions. Thus in order to make an actual decision now we have, at the same time, to make hypothetical decisions about the future. But, and this is the point, they are only hypothetical.

Perhaps an example will help. If a firm is to buy a new lorry this year, then it will have to decide whether to sell or keep it next year and in each subsequent year. It is obvious that the decision whether or not to buy it this year must partly depend upon expectations concerning the alternative future effects of exercising these alternative future options. Hypothetical decisions may have to be made now about when to get rid of the lorry in the future in order to decide what to do now. Thus analytically, a whole series of decisions is all made now. None the less, only one decision in this series is more than hypothetical, namely the first one.

This, I hope, is platitudinous. I have nevertheless spelt it out here in order to avoid having to mention it continually in what follows.

Talk of the planned load factor of AGR power stations in 1985, for example, does not commit one to an operating regime for the electricity system then; it is merely a question of working out what actions to take now.

An equally platitudinous consideration which needs to be borne in mind is that public enterprises exist. They can be expanded or contracted, but it would be wasteful to build a new one from scratch this year if an existing one has been inherited from last year. Hence talk about how costs would behave as a function of the size of a brand new one is pointless. This means that textbook long-run industry cost curves which reflect only today's technology and today's factor prices are no use. What matters are the costs of running and of expanding or contracting the hodge-podge we have got, the fossilization of past decisions taken by our predecessors.

The third consideration is that public enterprises normally know less about their demand than about their costs. Except for the rare cases where experimentation is possible, information about own-price and cross elasticities of demand is remarkably difficult to obtain for past years and still more difficult to predict for the future. This has an important implication for the way pricing can be done in practice. In principle, of course, the optimal price-output combination should be fixed in the light of predicted demand and cost functions. But when only point predictions of demand and rough guesses about elasticities are possible the only practical procedure is to proceed in steps:

1. Choose the relationship of prices to marginal costs which is most probably optimal;
2. Forecast demand in quantity terms;
3. Re-optimize production and investment plans;
4. Calculate marginal costs with output matching forecast demand;
5. Fix prices unless it is too soon since the last change;
6. Wait, while getting on with other tasks;
7. Go to step 2.

With this cycle there is feedback from prices to forecast demand, but it is not instantaneous. Since things change during step 6, no equilibrium or optimum may ever be reached. Life is like that, however, and one might as well try to adjust to it.

To sum up so far, the study of the costs of a public enterprise must be forward looking, reflecting hypothetical future decisions;

it must run in terms of maintaining, expanding or contracting an existing inherited productive apparatus, and it may have to apply to point output forecasts, ignoring the feedback via prices.

Given (i) a forecast time-stream of its outputs of this sort, (ii) its present assets and contracts, (iii) a set of expectations or assumptions both about future input prices and (iv) about technology, there is, for any public enterprise a time-stream of its current and hypothetically planned future inputs which will minimize the expected present worth of its avoidable costs. This can be calculated either, in principle at least, for time-streams stretching from now to infinity or, more practically, for a finite period. In the latter case, unless it is realistic to assume the dismantling of the enterprise at the terminal date, the device of crediting a terminal asset value frequently has to be used in working out an optimal time-stream of inputs. But this important practical consideration is irrelevant to the points to be made here, so it is convenient in what follows to talk as if expectations and plans stretch towards infinity. It is also convenient to suppose that the discount rate used for calculating present worths is constant and given and that there are no current or prospective constraints on expenditure which prevent the minimum cost solution from being chosen.

If, now, the forecast time-stream of outputs is changed by, say, increasing the output of product number 27 in 1981 from 2,900 to 2,901, the cost minimizing time-stream of inputs and the present worth of all avoidable costs will also change. This present worth will, of course, increase. Say it rises by £40. Then we define the present worth now of the marginal cost of product number 27 in 1981 as £40

If, alternatively, we use the discount rate to calculate the 1981 present worth of costs (compounding forward all earlier costs) we naturally get a higher figure, say £103. This is the 1981 present worth of the marginal cost of product number 27 in 1981. It may or may not be equal to the increase in 1981 costs. It will be equal if the cheapest way, planned now, of increasing the output in question involves the use of extra inputs only in that year. If, for example, hypothetical decisions involve spare capacity in 1981, and if higher capacity utilization then will not shorten the optimal life of capacity by wearing it out faster, then only extra labour and materials will be required. In this case, 1981 costs will change by £103 and the 1981 present worth of marginal cost is the same as the 1981 change in costs.

Where a change in capacity is involved, however, this is unlikely to be the case. The cheapest way, in present worth terms, of adjusting the time-stream of inputs to meet the altered output target may then involve input changes in other years besides 1981. It may, for example, involve building more capacity in 1980 or earlier. Alternatively, it may involve bringing forward some investment in new capacity from 1982 to 1981, thus actually decreasing costs to be incurred in 1982. Thus in general, the 1981 present worth of the marginal cost of a 1981 output is not the same thing as the change in 1981 costs.

We now have to note that this marginal cost will change as time marches on and we get nearer to 1981. One reason for this is obvious: plans and expectations may change. But there is another less obvious reason for change which may operate even if no plans or expectations alter. To show what it is, suppose that the optimal (i.e. the least-cost) method of adjusting inputs so as to add to 1981 output involves installing some new machines in 1978. Once we get past 1978 this can no longer be done. Hence a new, and necessarily dearer method of adjusting inputs must be resorted to, perhaps even a crash programme. More generally, in the absence of any divergence from the expectations and plans previously held, the 1981 present worth of 1981 marginal cost may rise and cannot fall as we approach 1981. The effluxion of time, that is to say, may eliminate certain options by changing them from future conditional to past definite.

In the absence of time, marginal cost (the derivative of total cost with respect to a particular output) is a simple concept. Now that time has been introduced it has become more complicated; for a unit change it is necessary to specify:

— the nature of the output,
— the timing of the change in it,
— the timing of the decision to change it,
— the date to which cost changes are discounted or compounded in calculating their present worth.

As an example, the 1972 present worth of the costs of a 1976 unit change in the output of product number 14 planned in 1971 is one possible combination. If we discount to obtain the present worth now of the cost change arising from an output change decided now, the answer will be called simply 'discounted marginal cost' in the rest of this chapter, but this must not be taken to mean that no discounting is required to calculate other marginal costs.

With such a multiplicity of marginal costs it is necessary to make sure which of them is relevant for pricing. Suppose that there are no constraints, externalities, income distribution issues or second-best problems whatsoever so that prices ought to equal marginal costs. The question 'Which marginal costs?' can then be answered by realizing that the purpose of marginal-cost pricing is to make the cost incurred or saved by the customer as a result of a decision reflect the cost incurred or saved by the public enterprise. Thus if his decision is to install a gas-fired kiln next year and use it for twenty years he should, ideally, be faced with a twenty-year schedule of the marginal costs of supplying him with the necessary gas, beginning next year and calculated with the decision to increase gas output made at the time when he decides to buy the kiln.

This requires an individual long-term contract with the single customer. Such contracts are only worth making with a few large customers, and even then some sort of average price will be calculated rather than one for each year. But the principle is clear. Where a customer's demand is large enough to justify the effort, a separate costing ought to be made of the demand he offers. Its amount and timing depend on him and it will not be marginal in the strict sense of relating to a tiny increment in output.

Otherwise, the problem is one of fixing a published price structure which is on offer to a very large number of customers. All of these customers are making very short-run decisions (switching on or off), while some of them are also making long-run decisions (buying or scrapping appliances), yet they cannot be distinguished and offered different prices. Furthermore, there will be some minimum period for which a new tariff or price list will have to endure – in the absence of totally unexpected and radical changes in costs or demand.

If a substantial change in marginal costs is expected to occur in a few years' time, this poses a dilemma. If, for example, because of indivisibilities, a new system is built with capacity in excess of the probable initial level of demand (as with a new natural gas pipeline system) marginal costs will be confined to running costs until demand has grown. Thus a price equalling initial marginal cost might attract some customers who would not choose to consume the product at the higher price that will follow. If they invest in new equipment to use the product they will subsequently realize that this investment was mistaken. For such customers, therefore, an initial price equal to the future, higher level of marginal cost (and thus well in excess of the initially lower level) may be required to avoid resource misallocation. Such a price may, however, choke off other, temporary sales which are worth while at the lower level. The appropriate initial price in such circumstances has to be chosen in such a way as to minimize the resulting waste.

Leaving aside such cases, consider the problem where a price structure which reflects marginal costs has to be fixed for a minimum period of *n* years starting now. Then it will have to reflect the average over the next *n* years of marginal costs in each of these years, each calculated in terms of decisions to change outputs made at the beginning of the year in question. (We are simplifying the exposition by speaking as though decisions are made only at and for yearly intervals.) Thus what is needed are such marginal cost estimates for each of the next *n* years starting now. Although as explained earlier, these may exceed the marginal costs of output changes decided upon in previous years there are cases where they will not.

The circumstances under which this will happen is one matter to be investigated. But there are others. What is the relation between the sum of the separate discounted marginal costs for a series of years and the single discounted marginal cost of a change in output spanning all those years? What is the relationship between marginal costs and $1/x$ of the cost of an output change of x units? Is there any concept of depreciation which fits into marginal cost? If so, what is its relationship to accountants' concepts of historical or replacement cost depreciation? When is marginal cost measured by the running cost of a particular portion of the public enterprise's capacity?

There are no general answers to these questions but I shall give answers in terms of a particular model which, though much simplified, possesses features which are to be found in quite a few actual cases. These answers and the concept of marginal costs are taken from articles by myself and Littlechild.[1] But they all relate to a sys-

[1] 'Marginal Cost' and 'Marginal Cost Pricing and Joint Costs' in *The Economic Journal*, June 1969 and June 1970 respectively. My article contains references to a number of important sources for the ideas it contains. Since then I have come across an admirable paper by H. R. Fisher, 'Obsolescence and Optimum Replacement Timing' which would have attracted more notice had it appeared elsewhere

tems approach and such a complex approach is not appropriate or necessary for all the activities of all public enterprises, so first its scope must be examined.

Many public enterprises can be thought of as consisting of three parts. First, there is the administration and such general functions as finance, marketing, personnel management, research and so on. Second, there is a complex central system whose planning and operation must take account of internal interrelationships. Third there is a multiplicity of fringe subsystems which interact with the central system but not with each other.

These second and third parts, on which attention is centred, have been rather vaguely defined, but some examples should make clear the distinction between them:

ENTERPRISE	CENTRAL SYSTEM	FRINGE SUB-SYSTEMS
Electricity	Generation and transmission	Distribution networks
Telephones	Exchanges and trunk network	Equipment and lines peculiar to individual subscribers
Airline	Planes, routes, timetables, maintenance, crew	Baggage and passenger handling etc. at each separate airport
Parcels	Major depots and trunk routes	Collection and delivery

The essential point about the analysis of central system costs, to which we now turn, is that figures of marginal costs should emerge as by-products of the search for a minimum cost solution since they are the duals of the demand constraints. A separate study of system costs is only necessary when system planning is not practised, either because it would be too complicated to be feasible or simply because top management does not believe in it.

As already explained, this point cannot be made and the questions about marginal costs cannot usefully be answered in general terms. So we shall examine them in the particular terms of as simple a system cost model as possible. The model chosen can be developed

than in *The Chemical Engineer*, April 1963. An interesting alternative approach in terms of control theory is to be found in M. Albouy and J. Nachtigal, 'Extension of the Marginal Cost Concept in Dynamic Economics', *European Economic Review*, spring 1970.

to fit real industries, which means that while the analysis lacks the superficial generality of formal neoclassical economic theory, its results are simplified versions of the sort of results relevant to a fairly wide range of systems.

Consider, then, an enterprise producing only one non-storable output. The demands it is to meet are given; thus the amount to be produced in period t is X_t and this has been decided in advance from $t = 0$ to infinity.

Output is produced only by one kind of 'capacity' which incurs running costs. The cost of new capacity may be expected to change through time however and so may the running costs per unit of output of new capacity. In addition, running costs may rise as capacity gets older. These costs are all externally determined and are recorded as given sets of values for all t and $t \geqslant v$ of:

c^v = the present worth now of the capital cost of a unit of new capacity which becomes operational in $t = v$.

r_t^v = the present worth now of the period t unit running cost of capacity which became operational in $t = v$.

The superscript v thus stands for the vintage of the capacity. So O_t^v means the output produced in period t by capacity of vintage v.

If, now, the number of units of capacity of vintage v is denoted by Q^v, the present worth of the total lifetime cost incurred in acquiring and using it is:

$$c^v \cdot Q^v + \sum_{t \geqslant v} r_t^v \cdot O_t^v$$

Summing over all vintages gives the present worth of the enterprise's total costs from now, $t = 0$, to infinity, an infinite horizon being chosen only to simplify the exposition:

$$\sum_{v \geqslant o} \left(c^v \cdot Q^v + \sum_{t \geqslant v} r_t^v \cdot O_t^v \right) \qquad (1)$$

Since we do not wish to confine the analysis to a new enterprise built from scratch, we can treat Q^0 as a given amount of capacity inherited from the past, $\bar{Q}^0$, and available free now at the beginning of period O so that $c^0 = 0$.

The objective function (1), is the present worth of system costs, which is to be minimized by choosing the best time-paths of capacity-acquisition Q^v and of operation O_t^v to provide the given time-path of output X_0, X_1, X_2, ... This minimization is subject to various constraints. These will now be set out as inequalities in a form suitable for their subsequent manipulation.

First, output from capacity of vintage v must be less than the amount of such capacity existing in year t:

$$O_t^v - Q^v \leqslant 0 \quad \text{for all } v \text{ and all } t \geqslant v \tag{2}$$

Note that Q^v does not carry a subscript because once that capacity is installed in $t = v$ it continues to be available, if wanted, in all subsequent years.

Second, the total outputs from capacity of all vintages existing in period t must not fall short of the specified output of the enterprise for that period. This requirement that demand be met holds for all t.

$$X_t - \sum_{v=o}^{t} O_t^v \leqslant 0 \tag{3}$$

Thirdly, the amount of capacity acquired (free) from previous periods cannot exceed the existing amount of such capacity:

$$Q^0 - \bar{Q}^0 \leqslant 0 \tag{4}$$

(Note the simplification of assuming that this capacity is homogeneous, with r_t^0 the same for all of it in any period t.)

Finally, capacity can be bought but not sold and it cannot produce a negative output, so for all v and all $t \geqslant v$,

$$Q^v, O_t^v \geqslant 0 \tag{5}$$

This does not, of course, mean that capacity will not be scrapped if it eventually becomes too expensive to run, but this will show up simply as $O_t^v = 0$ for periods after a certain time. (Scrap value is disregarded.)

We can now write the Lagrangian function to be minimized. Note that all the monetary terms in it are present worths. Using k_t^v as the multiplier for the capacity constraint (2), m_t as the multiplier for the output constraint (3) and u_0^0 as the multiplier for the existing-capacity constraint (4) the function is:

$$L(Q^v, O_t^v, k_t^v, m_t, u_0^0) = \sum_{v \geqslant o} \left(Q^v \cdot c^v + \sum_{t \geqslant v} O_t^v \cdot r_t^v \right)$$

$$+ k_t^v (O_t^v - Q^v) \quad \text{for all } v \text{ and } t \geqslant v$$

61

$$+ m_t\left(X_t - \sum_{v=o}^{t} O_t^v\right) \text{ for all } t$$

$$+ u_0^0(Q^0 - \bar{Q}^0) \tag{6}$$

The Kuhn-Tucker conditions for minimization can now be set out as follows in pairs where, in each pair, if one holds with strict inequality then the other holds with strict equality:

$$c^v - \sum_{t \geqslant v} k_t^v \geqslant 0 \quad ; \quad Q^v \geqslant 0 \quad \text{for all } v > 0 \tag{7}$$

$$- \sum_{t \geqslant o} k_t^o + u_0^0 \geqslant 0 \quad ; \quad Q^0 \geqslant 0 \tag{8}$$

$$r_t^v + k_t^v - m_t \geqslant 0 \quad ; \quad O_t^v \geqslant 0 \quad \text{for all } v \text{ and } t \geqslant v \tag{9}$$

$$O_t^v - Q^v \leqslant 0 \quad ; \quad k_t^v \geqslant 0 \quad \text{for all } v \text{ and } t \geqslant v \tag{10}$$

$$X_t - \sum_{v=o}^{t} O_t^v \leqslant 0 \quad ; \quad m_t \geqslant 0 \quad \text{for all } t \tag{11}$$

$$Q^0 - \bar{Q}^0 \leqslant 0 \quad ; \quad u_0^0 \geqslant 0 \tag{12}$$

(11) tells us that m_t will be positive whenever the required total output is produced, i.e. in all periods. Being the dual of the output constraint, m_t is the effect upon the objective function (1) of a unit change in X_t, the production required in period t. Since (1) is simply the present worth of system costs, it follows that m_t is the discounted marginal cost of period t, which is exactly what we are looking for.

(9) gives:

$$m_t = r_t^v + k_t^v \tag{13}$$

for capacity of all vintages which are actually used in period t, those for which $O_t^v > 0$. The r_t^v term is simple enough, as it is the discounted running cost. This alone equals m_t for that vintage of capacity which has a zero k_t^v, and (10) shows that this is the capacity which is not fully used, $O_t^v < Q^v$. Thus we have the simple result that whenever there is some vintage of capacity which is used but not fully, discounted marginal cost for that period equals its discounted running cost:

$$0 < O_t^v < Q^v \Rightarrow m_t = r_t^v \tag{14}$$

By the same token, (13) and (10) show that discounted marginal cost exceeds the discounted running cost of vintages of capacity which are fully utilized. The difference, k_t^v, is the discounted cost-saving from having an extra unit of capacity of vintage v in period t.

The Analysis of Marginal Costs

Since k_t^v is the dual of the capacity constraint (2), it measures the effect on the present worth of system costs of a unit change in the amount of capacity of that vintage in that period. Now this effect – the cost saving from having more capacity of a particular vintage – taken over the whole economic lifetime of the capacity is precisely what justifies acquiring that capacity in the first place. Hence it is that, according to (7):

$$Q^v > 0 \Rightarrow \sum_{t \geqslant v} k_t^v = c^v \qquad (15)$$

If the present worth of lifetime cost-savings (quasi-rents) were greater than c^v, this would mean that the acquisition of yet more capacity of vintage v would lower the present worth of system costs yet further. Hence cost minimization is inconsistent with such an excess. If, on the other hand, the present worth of lifetime cost savings is less than c^v, capacity of that vintage will not be acquired.

Finally, consider u_0^0, the dual of the existing capacity constraint. (12) shows that this will be positive when it is worthwhile using all of the capacity inherited from previous periods, capacity which we are assuming to be homogeneous. (8) shows that it is simply the sum of the discounted cost savings which its possession gives rise to. Thus the residual value of a unit of existing capacity at 0 is:

$$u_0^0 = \sum_{t \geqslant o} k_t^0 \qquad (16)$$

and it measures the increase in the present worth of system costs that would result were the amount of such capacity to be one unit less.

It may help the reader if we draw a diagram showing the relation between m_t, r_t^v and k_t^v for $t = 4$. The particular assumptions made in drawing it are that newer capacity has lower discounted running costs than older capacity and that total output required is growing through time. This diagram can be used in conjunction with another equation to discuss the inter-temporal interdependence of marginal costs. Combining (13) and (15) we get, for $Q^v > 0$:

$$\sum_{t \geqslant v} (m_t - r_t^v) = c^v$$

and using this, we can express m_4 for example as:

$$m_4 = r_4^4 + c^4 - \sum_{t \geqslant 5} (m_t - r_t^4) \qquad (17)$$

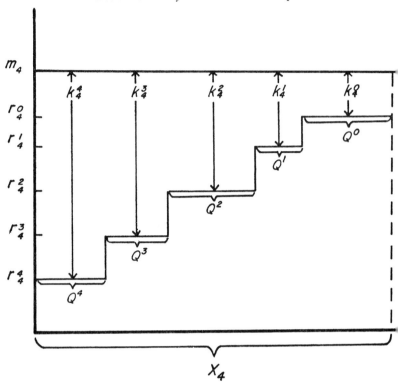

when $Q^4 > 0$. This shows clearly that discounted marginal cost for period 4 is related to discounted marginal cost in all the subsequent periods when the capacity of vintage 4 will continue to be used. Conversely, the discounted marginal cost for any of these subsequent periods is related to the discounted marginal cost for period 4. Thus while periods lying in the past affect marginal costs for future periods only via their legacy of $\bar{Q}^0$ capacity with running costs of r_t^0, outputs and marginal costs over a whole series of future periods are interdependent. m_t is *not* just a function of X_t.

In the diagram, which is drawn for an expanding enterprise where new capacity is cheaper to run than old capacity, discounted marginal cost for period 4 exceeds the discounted running cost of the oldest capacity: $m_4 > r_4^0$. This need not happen, of course; but the diagram has just been drawn that way. A unit increase in X_4 could be secured by making Q^4 one unit larger. This would make it possible to acquire one unit less of capacity of some later vintage. Hence the capital and running costs of later vintages as well as those of Q^4 affect the cost of the unit increase in output in period 4. These later costs also affect later marginal costs, and this explains why m_4 is related to the discounted marginal costs for subsequent periods and why they are related to it.

When conditions are such that new capacity is acquired in all periods, discounted marginal cost can in fact be viewed as the effect on the present worth of system costs of bringing forward or postponing the acquisition of one unit of capacity for one period. To see this, take (17) which shows discounted marginal cost to be the discounted running cost of new capacity plus the excess of its discounted capital cost over the present worth of its cost-savings in future periods, and re-write it as:

$$m_4 = c^4 + r_4^4 - (m_5 - r_5^4) - \sum_{t \geqslant 6} (m_t - r_t^4) \tag{17a}$$

Similarly, we have:

$$m_5 = c^5 + r_5^5 - (m_6 - r_6^5) - \sum_{t \geqslant 7} (m_t - r_t^5) \tag{17b}$$

Substituting (17b) for m_5 in (17a) and rearranging then gives:

$$m_4 = c^4 + \sum_{t \geqslant 4} r_t^4 - \left(c^5 + \sum_{t \geqslant 5} r_t^5 \right) \tag{18}$$

This is the present worth of the capital and lifetime running costs of an extra unit of vintage 4 capacity less the present worth of the capital and lifetime running costs saved by dispensing with one unit of vintage 5 capacity. But to acquire one more unit of capacity in period 4 and one less in period 5 is to bring forward the acquisition of a unit of capacity by one period. This demonstrates, then, that when new capacity is acquired in two successive periods, marginal cost in the first of them is the effect on system costs of bringing forward the acquisition of new capacity by one period, including the running cost of using it in the earlier period.

A similar argument can show that if old capacity is scrapped in all periods, discounted marginal cost is also the effect on the present worth of system costs of postponing scrapping it by one period, including the discounted running cost of using it in the later period. This fits in with the first approach. If system costs are minimized, the effect on them either of bringing forward or of postponing replacement (i.e. of simultaneous acquisition and scrapping) must be zero.

E

We can now look at the relationship between the increase in the present worth of system costs for a one-period unit output increase, m_t, and the increase resulting from a unit output increase extending over a number of periods. It turns out that the m_t are additive on present assumptions. Thus if the increase starts in period 4, it can be achieved by acquiring an extra unit of vintage 4 capacity and by not reducing acquisitions in subsequent periods until the unit output increase terminates. If, for example, the increase extends over periods 4–6, the effect on the present worth of costs $m_{4/6}$ is:

$$m_{4/6} = c^4 + \sum_{t \geqslant 4} r_t^4 - \left(c^7 + \sum_{t \geqslant 7} r_t^7 \right) \tag{19}$$

Comparison with (18) makes it clear that:

$$m_{4/6} = m_4 + m_5 + m_6$$

If the duration of a multi-period unit output increase happens to coincide with the optimal lifetime of new capacity coming into operation when the increase starts then there is no reduction in subsequent acquisitions. Thus if the increase is from $t = p$ to $t = q$:

$$m_{p/q} = c^p + \sum_{t = p}^{q} r_t^p$$

which, from (17) can be seen to equal:

$$\sum_{t = p}^{q} m_t.$$

Is there similar additivity when capacity is not being increased in all periods? If we take a number of consecutive such periods and if we suppose that there is some spare capacity in all of them, then the answer is obviously in the affirmative. Only if an extra unit of output would require an extra unit of capacity when the increment in output starts and new capacity would not otherwise have been acquired will this not be the case. The marginal cost at such a position will then be greater for an increment than for a decrement in output.

The answer to the question about the relationship between unit marginal cost, and $1/x$ of the extra costs of an extra x units runs along similar lines. If capacity is being acquired in all periods and the increment in output applies to all periods, then the two are equal. This follows from the assumptions of linearity and divisibility.

But if one or other of these conditions is not met no general answer is possible.

We have now shown the nature of discounted marginal cost in terms of the simple model. It is clear that it emerges from the set of hypothetical decisions designed to minimize the present worth of the future costs of providing a given time-stream of output. A change in the required time-stream or in the discount rate or in the expected future values of capital and running costs will require re-optimization and will yield a new set of marginal costs. At each successive re-optimization, the capacity acquisitions which were planned last time and have since been undertaken become part of existing capacity. The amount they cost loses relevance to decision-making and to the calculation of marginal costs, but they acquire a residual value, u, which emerges from the calculations.

Let us return to the case where re-optimization is not necessary because expectations do not change and consider the significance of k_t^v. This, it will be recalled, is the present worth of the dual for period t of the vintage v capital constraint and measures the loss or gain that would arise were one less or one more unit of that capacity to be available in that period. Let us call it discounted 'amortization'.

The equation:

$$Q^v > 0 \Rightarrow \sum_{t \geqslant v} k_t^v = c^v \tag{15}$$

can now be interpreted as saying that the present worth of lifetime amortization equals the discounted capital cost of new capacity which is acquired.

The equation:

$$m_t = r_t^v + k_t^v \quad \text{for all } v \text{ and } t \geqslant v \tag{13}$$

says that discounted marginal cost in period t equals discounted running cost in that period plus discounted amortization in that period for capacity of all vintages then in use.

Consider a period $t = 8$ when some new capacity is put into operation and when capacity of vintage 3 first permanently ceases to be used. Vintage 8 capacity is thus replacing vintage 3 capacity. From (10) $k_8^8 > 0$ and $k_8^3 = 0$. Hence (9) gives:

$$m_8 = r_8^8 + k_8^8 < r_8^3$$

Thus replacement takes place when the discounted first-year running cost and first-year amortization of new capacity falls below the discounted running cost of old capacity.

The present worth of the residual value of capacity at the beginning of any period, generalizing (16) is:

$$u_t^v = \sum_{j \geqslant t} k_j^v \tag{20}$$

Hence $k_t^v = u_t - u_{t+1}$.

If we use i to indicate the discount rate and capital letters to denote undiscounted values, this can be written:

$$\frac{K_t^v}{(1+i)^{t+1}} = \frac{U_t}{(1+i)^t} - \frac{U_{t+1}}{(1+i)^{t+1}} \tag{21}$$

where K_t^v relates to the end of period t, not the beginning. Multiplying through by $(1+i)^{t+1}$ gives:

$$K_t^v = U_t - U_{t+1} + iU_t \tag{22}$$

This says that (undiscounted) amortization for vintage v in period t equals the fall in the residual value per unit of capacity during period t plus interest on residual value at the beginning of the period. Thus if the fall in residual value is called 'Depreciation':

Amortization = 'Depreciation' + Interest

'Depreciation' has been put in inverted commas because it will only equal accounting depreciation in period t by a fluke. Similarly, Interest being interest on residual value, it will equal interest on book value only by a fluke.

Since the residual value of new capacity is its capital cost and the residual value of capacity which is being replaced is zero, the undiscounted sum of planned lifetime 'Depreciation' will equal capital cost. The same is, of course, true of accounting depreciation if, as here, scrap value is ignored. But the time pattern of the two can well differ very widely. While accounting depreciation is determined by some simple rule – straight-line, diminishing balance, etc. – and by an arbitrary choice of life, 'Depreciation' is the result of an explicit optimization calculation. Using capital letters again to denote undiscounted values, we have, from (13):

$$K_t^v = M_t - R_t^v \tag{23}$$

Since K_t^v must start positive and end up at zero, it must generally fall through time, though it may go down to zero in periods during its life when the capacity in question is temporarily not fully utilized and then rise again. R_t^v will presumably rise steadily as the capacity gets older, while the development of marginal cost through time reflects the evolution of the capital and running costs of subsequent vintages of capacity.

Since lifetime 'Depreciation' equals capital cost it will equal replacement cost if, and only if, replacement cost equals original cost. There is no general presumption that this will be the case. Thus the effect on marginal costs of any expected changes in the capital cost of future vintages of capacity can only be studied via the optimization calculation. It is, of course, true that, other things being equal, a higher capital cost of future vintages will make for higher marginal costs in some of the intervening periods. But the magnitude and timing of the increases cannot be calculated in terms of any excess of replacement cost depreciation over original cost depreciation. It is tempting to suppose that such a short-cut exists, but it does not.

All that has been said so far about amortization related to the set of expectations and hypothetical decisions holding good at the time the capacity was acquired. Once a change occurs in the planned time stream of outputs, or in the discount rate or in expected future capital and running costs then, as already pointed out, a re-optimization becomes necessary. This will yield a new set of marginal costs and, from (23), will thus produce a new series of K_t^v from then on for existing capacity. The residual value of this capacity will thus rise or fall according to whether this new series has a higher or lower present worth than the old one had. Lifetime 'Depreciation' will then turn out to exceed or fall short of capital cost. We can call the difference 'Obsolescence' if we wish, and say that 'Depreciation' plus 'Obsolescence' equals capital cost. Thus these terms can be given definitions which fit in with the concept of marginal cost as derived from optimization. It must be realized, however, that neither concept is in any way necessary either for the calculation of a set of optimal hypothetical decisions or for calculating the corresponding set of marginal costs. Furthermore, care must be taken to avoid confusion with the arbitrary notions of depreciation and obsolescence used in orthodox accounts.

This concludes the exposition, in terms of an extremely simple model, of various cost concepts in a dynamic systems analysis.

Similar concepts emerge in the analysis of real cases. It would be helpful if a parallel exemplary analysis of the cost structure of a multiplicity of fringe sub-systems could also be provided. Unfortunately I can think of no suitable model. But this merely means that there is no equally useful set of concepts, not that individual cases cannot be analysed. The point is that no one type of programming model is suitable; in some cases, indeed, an inductive approach is required. Chapter 6 of my *Optimal Pricing and Investment in Electricity Supply* outlines one example. Before getting down to examples in this book, however, there is a little more theory to be expounded.

7

OPTIMAL PRICING THROUGH TIME

Now that we have a marginal cost concept which is dynamic, let us go back from minimizing costs to maximizing Benefit less Costs. As explained in the last chapter, since cost optimization models are much more feasible than quantitative demand studies, the practical derivation of prices which maximize Benefits less Costs is difficult or impossible. Iteration through time from sales forecasts to cost-minimization to price-fixing and back to sales forecasts is therefore necessary. But as maximizing Benefits minus Costs in a simultaneous analysis is the ideal from which we fall short, it is best to use it for thinking about questions of principle. This chapter is about some such principles.

Once again, in order to concentrate on some issues it is best to neglect others. The complications dealt with in earlier chapters are thus all ignored and no relevant constraints upon maximization are brought in.

We shall use the model of the last chapter, introducing a demand function. Let

$$p_t = p_t\left(\sum_{v=0}^{t} O_t^v\right)$$

be the inverse demand function giving discounted price in period t as a function of output in that period. There is such a function for each period and they are treated as independent of one another in the sense that price in any one period is unrelated to outputs in other periods.

Integrating over total output to obtain willingness to pay, the objective function to be maximized is:

$$\underbrace{\sum_{t \geq 0} \int_0^{\Sigma O^v} p_t\left(\sum_{v=o}^{t} O_t^v\right) d \sum_{v=o}^{t} O_t^v}_{\text{Benefits}} - \underbrace{\sum_{v \geq o}\left(c^v \cdot Q^v + \sum_{t \geq v} r_t^v \cdot O_t^v\right)}_{\text{Costs}}$$

Since this is now a maximization problem, the constraints are best written as 'not less than', but retain their meanings unchanged. First there is the capacity constraint, whose dual is k_t^v:

$$Q^v - O_t^v \geq 0 \quad \text{for all } v \text{ and } t \geq v \tag{2}$$

There is no output constraint this time, since output is now endogenous, but the third constraint (on the amount of capacity inherited from the past) remains with its dual u_0^0:

$$\bar{Q}^0 - Q^0 \geq 0 \tag{3}$$

Finally, capacity can be bought but not sold and output cannot be negative:

$$Q^v, O_t^v \geq 0$$

The Kuhn-Tucker conditions for maximization can now be set out, in an order comparable with (7)–(12) in the last chapter:

$$\sum_{t \geq v} k_t^v - c^v \leq 0 \quad ; \quad Q^v \geq 0 \quad \text{for all } v > 0 \tag{4}$$

which means that discounted lifetime quasi-rents equal the discounted capital cost of newly acquired capacity.

$$u_0^0 - \sum_{t \geq o} k_t^0 \leq 0 \quad ; \quad Q^0 \geq 0 \tag{5}$$

which gives the residual value of existing capacity inherited from the past.

$$p_t - r_t^v - k_t^v \leq 0 \quad ; \quad O_t^v \geq 0 \quad \text{for all } v \text{ and } t \geq v \tag{6}$$

$$Q^v - O_t^v \geq 0 \quad ; \quad k_t^v \geq 0 \quad \text{for all } v \text{ and } t \geq r \tag{7}$$

which shows that capacity which is not fully used has a zero k_t^v.

$$\bar{Q}^0 - Q^0 \geq 0 \quad ; \quad u_0^0 \geq 0 \tag{8}$$

Comparison with the last chapter shows only one significant difference, namely that for $O^v > 0$, from (6):

$$p_t = r_t^v + k_t^v$$

instead of:

$$m_t = r_t^v + k_t^v$$

This suggests that, under the assumptions made, marginal-cost pricing maximizes Benefits less Costs. As we shall see, however, this is too simple a way of putting it, though it is not fundamentally incorrect.

A distinction is sometimes drawn between 'long-run' and 'short-run' marginal-cost pricing. Unfortunately it is not always clear just what this means; 'short-run' can have various meanings, in particular:

(a) planned at short notice;
(b) starting soon;
(c) lasting for a short time;
(d) achieved by altering capacity utilization rather than capacity.

In the light of this multiplicity of meanings it may be safer to eschew the use of the distinction altogether.

The relation of optimal price to running costs and to the amount of capacity in any period (assuming that price is not constrained from period to period changes) will be that shown in one of the two accompanying diagrams, where DD is the relevant demand curve.

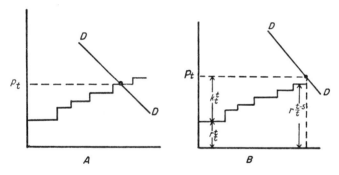

In case A, price equals the running cost of the capacity not fully utilized.

In case B, $p_t = m_t = r_t^t + k_t^t$, i.e. the running cost and first-year amortization of the capacity first coming into operation during the period. Alternatively, the price in case B can be described as that which will restrict demand to equal capacity output. So long as the amount of new capacity brought into operation in period t is capable of variation, the equivalence of these two statements follows from the fact that optimal decisions have been taken.

As t approaches, however, the amount of new capacity will cease to be variable: the hypothetical decision becomes an actual decision and from then on it is too late to do anything about it. It is now awkward to say that price equals marginal cost; marginal cost of an output decrease in t is now less than price, being r_t^{t-5}, and the marginal cost of an output increase is now infinitely greater than price. It is still true that the optimal price is that which restricts demand to capacity output, but the only marginal cost which it equals is the historic one of a unit change in output planned in the past. Furthermore, it will equal this marginal cost only if the demand curve and costs are just as they were expected to be when the amount of new capacity of vintage t was finally decided. If expectations have changed since then, necessitating re-optimization, the new price for period t will not even equal this marginal cost. But it will still be such as to restrict demand to capacity output.

The only statement which it is strictly proper to make, therefore, is that:

1. In each period price is whichever is the greater of:
   (a) the running cost of that capacity which is partly utilized, or
   (b) the level required to restrict demand to capacity.
2. The amount of new capacity decided upon to come into operation in any period, if positive, is such as to make its expected $\sum_{t \geqslant v} k_t^v$ equal its c^v per unit.
3. Planned discounted price equals planned discounted marginal cost in all future periods except those where new capacity is to come into operation in an amount which is now irrevocably determined.

If we wish to continue using the terms 'short-run' and 'long-run' while avoiding their ambiguous use as qualifiers of 'marginal cost', we can call (1) the 'short-run pricing rule' and (2) the 'long-run investment rule'.

These rules are not, however, completely general, but apply only under present assumptions. If, for example, demand is stochastic within a period,[1] if price has to be fixed for more than one period or if stocks can be accumulated, then more complicated rules will apply. Thus the principles set out, like those in previous chapters, are only simple examples of an approach to optimization. Each particular public enterprise has its own particular conditions relevant to optimal pricing and investment.

---

[1] For a discussion of how not to approach this complication see my note 'Public Utility Pricing and Output under Risk: Comment', *The American Economic Review*, Vol. LX, No. 3, June 1970.

The above programming formulation of optimal multi-period pricing and investment in equations (1)–(8) follows Littlechild.[2] We now follow him further to demonstrate the isomorphism of this analysis with that of joint costs and peak pricing.

In order to do this, consider a simpler version of the model where all capacity is acquired at the beginning and there is a finite number of periods, n. Thus the v superscript disappears and the objective function to be maximized is simply:

$$\sum_{t=o}^{n}\int^{O_t} p_t(O_t)dO_t - \left(c \cdot Q + \sum_{t=o}^{n} r_t \cdot O_t\right)$$

The capacity constraint, with the multiplier k_t, is now:

$$Q - O_t \geqslant 0 \quad \text{for } t = 0 \ldots n \tag{10}$$

and the non-negativity constraint is:

$$Q, O_t \geqslant 0 \quad \text{for } t = 0 \ldots n \tag{11}$$

The Kuhn-Tucker conditions now reduce to:

$$\sum_{t=o}^{n} k_t - c \leqslant 0 \quad ; \quad Q \geqslant 0 \quad \text{for } t = 0 \ldots n \tag{12}$$

$$p_t - r_t - k_t \leqslant 0 \quad ; \quad O_t \geqslant o \quad \text{for } t = 0 \ldots n \tag{13}$$

$$Q - O_t \geqslant 0, \, k_t \geqslant 0 \quad \text{for } t = 0 \ldots . n \tag{14}$$

In interpreting this algebra we can think of $O_0, O_1, O_2 .. O_n$ in any of three ways:

(i) As before, except that the outputs of the single product are produced by only one initial vintage of capacity, with a unit capital cost of c, for only n periods stretching into the future;

(ii) As the outputs produced during a year in each of n periods into which the year is divided, using capacity with an annual cost of c.

(iii) As n different outputs produced simultaneously by capacity.

For example, in case (ii) the year might be divided simply into a high-demand and a low-demand period, while in case (iii) Q units of capacity will produce up to Q units of O_0 (at a unit separate cost of r_0), up to Q units of O_1 (at a unit separate cost of r_1) and so on.

---

[2] 'Marginal Cost Pricing with Joint Costs', *The Economic Journal*, Vol. LXXX, June 1970.

Case (ii), it will be seen, is a simple analysis of peak pricing. In peak periods $p_t = r_t + k_t$ and the sum of $p_t - r_t$ over such periods just covers c. Case (iii) on the other hand, is a simple analysis of joint costs. Those outputs which sell at more than their separate costs jointly contribute enough to cover c, while any whose output falls short of Q merely cover their own separate costs.

If $n = 2$, the analysis can be put into a simple diagrammatic form, following Steiner's classic paper on peak pricing.[3] The downward sloping curve in the bottom diagram is derived from the demand and separate cost curves for 0 and 1 in the top two diagrams. It shows $[p_0(O_0) - r_0] + [p_1(O) - r_1]$ for $O_0 = O_1$ and $p_t \geqslant r_t$ and can be called the 'demand for capacity curve'. As drawn, the demand for O_0 is low and the whole of c is included in p_1.

Thus, if Q is a ship running in winter, 0, and summer, 1, the winter price, p_0, merely covers winter running costs and in winter there is $Q - O_0$ unused capacity. If Q is a kiln producing seconds, 0, and perfects, 1, only O_0 of the seconds will be processed at a unit cost of r_0.

Neither of these examples is completely satisfactory but once again it would be unreasonable to expect a simple model to provide answers for real cases. The point has been made, nevertheless, that jointness over time is fundamentally similar to jointness between products.

We can now take another look at the concept of marginal cost. m_t, discounted marginal cost, has been defined as the effect on the present worth of total system costs of a unit change in O_t, given all other O. Littlechild calls this 'ceteris paribus marginal cost' and points out that there is another concept relevant to optimal pricing, which he calls 'mutatis mutandis marginal cost'.

Suppose that plans are changed and that O_t is increased by one unit. If this involves the acquisition of more capacity to come into operation in period t it is possible that other O will change too. If they do; if, that is to say, there is some consequential effect upon the optimal O for other periods; then the 'ceteris paribus marginal cost' will not describe the full effects of the unit change in O_t. Thus suppose that a capacity increase of one unit in period t is followed neither by smaller capacity acquisitions, nor by a saving in running costs in

[3] 'Peak Loads and Efficient Pricing', *Quarterly Journal of Economics*, Vol. 71, November 1957.

some later period, $t+j$, but by an increase in output. Then the effect on the objective function with respect to this later period is:

$$k_{t+j}^t = p_{t+j} - r_{t+j}^t$$

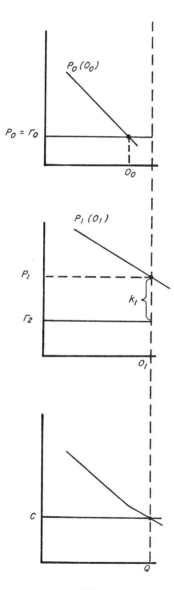

Clearly, k_{t+j}^t here reflects an increase in Benefits less Costs, not a decrease in Costs. Hence in the equation we get by combining (4) and (6):

$$p_q = c^q + r_q^q - \sum_{t>q} k_t^q \qquad (15)$$

the interpretation of k^q differs somewhat from that in the corresponding cost-minimization result obtainable from the last chapter:

$$m_q = c^q + r_q^q - \sum_{t>q} k_t^q \qquad (16)$$

In (15), some of the k_t^q relate to an increase in output, while in (16) all of them relate to cost savings. The right hand side of (15) is what Littlechild calls 'mutatis mutandis marginal cost' while the right hand side of (16) is his 'ceteris paribus marginal cost'.

Their relationship can be seen most clearly if we take the joint-cost case of cattle which provide both beef, b, and hides, h, and if we assume that all of both are fully utilized. This assumption, namely:

$$O_b = O_h = Q$$

from (14) means that both k_b and k_h are positive, so (12) and (13) give:

$$k_b + k_h = c$$
$$p_b = r_b + k_b$$
$$p_h = r_h + k_h$$

The 'ceteris paribus marginal cost' of beef,

$$m_b = c + r_b$$

is the whole of the extra costs incurred when the output of hides is kept constant. The 'mutatis mutandis marginal cost' however,

$$p_b = c + r_b - k_h$$

is the extra cost *minus* the gain in Benefits less Cost to be had from utilizing the extra hides provided by the extra cattle necessary to provide the extra beef.

If, as we should, we accept Littlechild's concepts but, as hitherto, stick to using 'marginal cost' only in the 'ceteris paribus' sense as derived from cost minimization, then we cannot describe optimal prices as all equalling marginal costs. But, as we saw earlier in the chapter when formulating the pricing and investment rules, there are other reasons supporting this conclusion. 'Marginal-cost pricing' may be a useful shorthand for unconstrained 'Benefit-less-Cost — maximizing pricing' but it is not wholly accurate. The 'short-term pricing rule' and the 'long-run investment rule' are a better way of summarizing our principles for the simple model.

8

URBAN PUBLIC TRANSPORT

Financial problems are frequently pressing in large cities. Formally speaking, this means that financial constraints are relevant and important. Since such constraints are fairly obvious the economist may sometimes need to stress that social benefits and costs are important too. The following remarks, which relate to pricing and investment decisions that have to be taken by the London Transport Executive (LTE), start off in this way.[1]

Decisions to increase fares or reduce services cannot be taken by reference to the LTE's financial position only. The effect on the LTE's passengers obviously needs to be considered too; less obviously the effect on other groups – such as those who might be inconvenienced by greater road congestion – must also be considered. Thus, for a full analysis of the possible consequences of any change, estimates need to be made not only of the effects on the LTE's costs and revenues but also of the social costs and benefits, i.e. of costs and benefits to society as a whole. The costs and benefits are the sum of the effects on the LTE, its passengers, and any other sectors of society affected by the change. Thus the (financial) effects on the LTE are not a separate set of considerations but are one part of the effects that need to be looked at. The LTE and the GLC, who are responsible for taking these decisions, are of course well aware of the kinds of analyses that are required, but the subject is one that affects the public generally and a more general discussion is warranted.

When a particular choice would both improve LTE's financial position and raise social benefits more (or lower them less) than costs, the case for that choice is clear. Difficulty arises when the

[1] The rest of this chapter reproduces Chapter 4 and Appendix G of *London Transport Fares*, Report 159 of The National Board for Prices and Incomes (HMSO Cmnd. 4540, November 1970); reproduced with the permission of the Controller of Her Majesty's Stationery Office.

financial effects on LTE point in one direction and the balance of social benefits points in the other. This, unfortunately, is the position with many of the decisions which have to be made.

A minor example will illustrate the point. It is estimated that suspending a specimen suburban bus service would lose the LTE £29,000 in annual revenue but save annual costs of £68,000 thus improving its financial position by £39,000. Looked at from the point of view of society as a whole, however, there would be a loss in that the estimated saving in Social Costs falls short of the estimated loss of Social Benefits by £87,000.

On a larger scale too there are changes in bus services which would improve LTE's financial position considerably but whose consequences for society as a whole might well be adverse. For example, the Red Arrow buses, although providing an essential service, are nevertheless operating at a loss even with a 4p fare.

Hence, before taking decisions, there is a need for an examination of the social costs and benefits of the alternatives which are open. These include general or selective fare increases, cutting the services or carrying on as at present (in which case it has to be decided who will pay).

It would be misleading to suggest that cost-benefit analysis of such options can solve any particular problem. It cannot; all it can do is to illuminate it. Its function is to set out in a systematic way those relevant considerations which are quantifiable to help management. It is an aid to decision-making, not a substitute for it.

Some of the considerations relevant to any decision cannot reasonably be expressed in monetary terms. While the development of techniques of analysis will extend the range which can, there will always remain others which cannot. Some amenity considerations are an example. Thus while cost-benefit calculations are necessary, they are not sufficient and need to be accompanied by a description of the other factors if management is to be presented with all the facts and arguments which are relevant.[2] This must be done with great care, however. It is all too easy for the proponents of a particular alternative to describe certain of its advantages in words which restate items that are already included in the figures so that these items get counted twice over.

The classic example of this fallacy is to accompany an estimate of

[2] An example is provided by Chapter 7, 'The Unquantified Factors', in the Ministry of Transport Publication, *Report of a Study of Rail Links with Heathrow Airport* (HMSO 1970).

the gain to generated traffic by a description of the gain in prosperity in an area, as a result of improved access, as though these were two entirely different things. At least part of this gain is merely the reflection of the new traffic. Thus if, for example, rents rise near a new Underground station this is in part a passing-on to landlords of benefits enjoyed by travellers. Though very relevant to the question of distribution between different groups it is not wholly an additional benefit. Similarly, it is true that an improvement in accessibility may improve job availabilities in an area and lead more people to travel to work there. These people clearly benefit. But care must be taken to avoid double-counting this benefit by including it both as a benefit to new travellers into the area and as a benefit to the same people in their role as workers.

Returning to the considerations which can be estimated in quantitative terms, we have tried to find out how much is being done to apply existing techniques and to improve them. Many of the techniques and measurements required apply to other transport problems besides those of London; for example the values to be assigned to savings or losses in passengers' time by lengthening or shortening journeys have been estimated by the Ministry of Transport and are used in a variety of contexts.

One important and difficult problem in analysing costs and benefits in transport is the analysis of 'modal choice', i.e. of the factors affecting the choice of mode of transport. A proposed improvement in availability or convenience or a reduction in fares on one means of transport will attract passengers from other means of transport, and conversely. These effects have to be predicted. Thus the effect of a new Underground line in attracting passengers from cars and buses and the effect of a bus fare increase in causing passengers to shift over to trains and cars must be estimated as part of any cost-benefit analysis of a new line or of a fare increase. A major issue, when such possibilities are examined, is the effect they will have on commuter car traffic and hence on road congestion. Thus, to take the case of a new Underground line, an important part of the social benefits would consist of the easing of road congestion resulting from car commuters shifting to the Underground.

What is required, then, is first the measurement of existing passenger flows by the various transport modes and, secondly, a means of predicting how they will change. The resulting estimates of the effects of the proposal then serve as one of the bases of the financial and cost-benefit calculations. We describe in Appendix F[3] the techniques currently used by the LTE for forecasting the traffic on a new Underground line, techniques which are equally relevant to analysing the effects of closing part of an existing line. Although it is clear that LTE makes its estimates with admirable thoroughness and imagination on the basis of all the methods and data currently available, it is also clear that firmer support for the estimates of the number of passengers shifting over from road transport would be helpful.

A similar need is obvious in relation to the question of whether or not peak-pricing should be introduced by LTE.[4] Peak demand is concentrated on many routes in as little as one mile out of the whole and the time taken on the route is sometimes such that each bus can traverse this crucial segment only once during each peak period. Thus taking fifty passengers as a load, each extra fifty passenger miles in a peak period in the peak direction over such a segment will require the provision of an additional bus. With two peak periods per working day and 255 working days in the year, the additional bus can provide 25,500 peak passenger miles per annum over the crucial distance. The corresponding addition to London Transport's costs per annum is about £6,400 (at autumn 1970 wage and price levels) for a double-deck two-man operated bus (the corresponding sum for a one-man operated bus would be lower) made up as follows:

	£ *per* *annum*
Crew wages, bonuses and related pension and national insurance contributions (on the basis of one crew with a maximum duty period)	3,900[5]
Fuel, tyres and maintenance related to performance of mileage	450
Overhaul, repairs, cleaning, lubricating and servicing	850
Vehicle licences	50
	5,250
Economic cost of the vehicle[6] (interest at 10 per cent and capital repayment charge over life of, say, 16 years)	1,150
	6,400

[3] Not reproduced here.

[4] This paragraph briefly repeats the argument of Appendix 3 of our Report No. 112, where the concepts are explained, but includes revised figures.

[5] This is a minimum.

[6] Estimated current replacement value of a bus (ignoring for this purpose the receipt of a bus grant) – £9,000 – being the original cost of a Routemaster bus uplifted by reference to price indices.

The marginal cost of the bus per peak passenger mile over the crucial distance is therefore roughly 25p compared with a fare of only $2\frac{1}{2}$p a mile for most journeys. However if a substantial proportion of passengers were induced to shift over to using private cars as a result of peak pricing, the resulting increase in congestion on the roads might well add to society's costs more than was saved by the reduction in peak bus traffic. Thus it is very important to know how a change in bus (and train) fares will affect people's choices of their mode of travel to work.

Research into these matters can follow either of two lines. One is the estimation of what are called 'diversion curves' and multiple-variable elaborations of them. (These involve the analysis of aggregative travel flows.) The other is the study of the travel choices made by a sample of individuals which either compares what each person did before and after a change or which compares each person's usual mode with his next best alternative. A considerable amount of academic research has been carried out on these lines over the last five years or so, and indeed such a study is under way at the Ministry of Transport. Before and after the British Rail fare increase of April 26, 1970, questionnaires were issued to employees in a sample of thirty-three large organizations in central London. Some 22,000 and 15,000 usable responses, respectively, were obtained giving information on the journey to work and, on the second occasion, about alternative methods of travel as well. A matching up of questionnaires in the two surveys to identify people who changed their mode of travel will, it is hoped, yield information about the effect of the rail fare increase, although experience suggests that before and after studies are difficult to handle. Information from the second survey concerning the choice between the mode of travel chosen and the alternative will also be analysed. Since the survey is by far the largest of this sort so far undertaken in Britain and since advanced mathematical techniques will be applied in the analyses, this is a welcome and promising step.[7] However, there still remain difficulties in translating the findings of relatively academic research such as this into operational procedures for predicting the consequences of particular future fare increases, or into general insights for management about the general behaviour of their markets.

[7] The survey implements a suggestion made in Chapter 2, Report No. 137 – *Proposals by the British Railways Board for Fare Increases in the London Commuter Area* (Cmnd. 4250, December 1969).

We also note the introduction in August 1970 of a 1p differential between peak and off-peak prices in Manchester and Salford and hope that studies of its effects will be useful in a national, as well as a local, context.

Modal choice analysis, as explained above, is part of the process of predicting the effect upon traffic flows of a change in the system, a fare alteration, or whatever constitutes the problem in hand. Thus it is only one step in the analysis of social costs and benefits. We have described all the steps in one relatively simple case in Appendix E.[8] The 'Report of a Study of Rail Links with Heathrow Airport' referred to in footnote 2 describes a much more complicated analysis. We have not attempted to review all aspects of the state of the art in general, but now pick out one particular topic on which we have some points to make.

Extra traffic on the roads slows down existing traffic, thus imposing costs both in the form of extra time lost and in the form of extra vehicle running costs. Conversely, the diversion of traffic from the roads reduces costs for the remaining traffic. Thus it is necessary to establish quantitative measures of the change in delay resulting from a change in traffic flow. This used to be done using a speed-flow formula, but this approach does not apply to delays at intersections which are used to capacity. Since the latter are considered to be the more important during the rush hours in central London, the LTE has applied in cost-benefit studies a different approach (developed by the Ministry of Transport) which concentrates on intersections. While this fails to bring into account the interactions between intersections in a network, it may represent an improvement. Unfortunately the parameters of the formula have not been measured and have so far been based on little more than guesswork when the formula has been applied. However, an alternative formulation is possible which would drastically simplify measurement and allow calculations to be made for particular routes. In the following paragraphs we explain the existing approach and our own reformulation.

The aim is to calculate the effects of additional vehicle journeys upon the time taken for existing vehicle journeys. The delay cost and extra operating costs caused by this extra congestion can then be estimated. Here we consider only the first step, the Ministry of Transport's method of calculating the extra time.

[8] This Appendix, not reproduced here, describes a cost-benefit analysis of the withdrawal of a suburban bus route.

In the crowded centre of London and the congested 'glue-pot ring' (as London Transport and the Ministry call it) around the central area, additional traffic will both slow down speeds along streets between intersections and increase waiting time at intersections. But the first of these effects can be neglected because a vehicle which takes an extra minute to get from the exit from one intersection to the back of the queue of vehicles waiting to cross the next intersection will merely wait one minute less when it gets there. Thus so long as there is no interaction between different intersections along a route in the shape of queues stretching the whole distance between them, the effect of extra traffic upon delays along it can be measured by concentrating upon the effect of the extra traffic at each intersection.

Once there is a queue at a branch of an intersection the hourly flow of traffic from that branch and across it has nothing to do with the length of the queue. Instead it depends on the layout of the intersection, the magnitude of the other traffic flows across the intersection, the pattern of turns and the phasing of the traffic lights – all of them independent of the length of the queue. Let this hourly flow, the capacity flow for the stream in question, be denoted C. It has the dimension of passenger car units per hour. A bus, for example, is given a p.c.u. value of $2\frac{1}{4}$, meaning that it adds to congestion $2\frac{1}{4}$ times as much as a car.

A queue starts to form once traffic starts to arrive at an hourly rate in excess of C. Suppose that over a period with a duration of t hours it arrives at an average hourly rate of $C+O$, never falling sufficiently below this average for the queue to dissipate. Then by the end of this period $t(C+O)$ will have arrived but only tC will have crossed the intersection so that a queue of tO will be waiting to cross. Since the queue started from nothing and ended up at tO, its average size over the whole period will be about half of tO, i.e. $tO/2$. The total amount of waiting (delay) involved is therefore $t^2O/2$, i.e. average size times the duration of the period.

Once the rate at which traffic arrives falls off from an average of O over capacity to a new level of U below it, the queue will begin to shrink. Traffic is now arriving at an hourly rate of $C-U$, so traffic will move out of the queue faster than new traffic joins the back of it at an hourly rate of U. As the queue rose to a maximum length of tO, the time taken for it to disappear will be tO/U. As it falls during this time from tO to zero, its average size is $tO/2$ as before and the delay involved therefore comes to:

$$\frac{tO}{2} \times \frac{tO}{U} = \frac{t^2O^2}{2U}.$$

The total amount of delay at the intersection to all the vehicles involved from the beginning to the disappearance of the queue thus comes out to: $t^2O/2 + t^2O^2/2U$. From this the increase in total delay to all vehicles which will result from the addition of one single extra p.c.u. during the whole period during which the hourly arrival rate is $C + O$ can be calculated. This is done by taking the first derivative with respect to O and then dividing by t to get: $t(1/2 + O/U)$.

Now this includes not only the delay suffered by all the existing traffic but also the delay suffered by the additional vehicle itself. This must therefore be subtracted in order to get the extra delay imposed on the existing traffic, the marginal congestion costs.

On average, an additional vehicle which joins the queue during the t hours when the flow is $C + O$ will arrive halfway through. Hence the number of p.c.u.s in the queue in front of it will be $tO/2$. Since the capacity of the intersection is C p.c.u.s per hour, each p.c.u. takes on average $1/C$ of an hour to cross it. Thus the additional vehicle will have to wait $(tO/2) \times (1/C)$ until it can cross; i.e. it suffers a delay of $tO/2C$. This then is what has to be subtracted to give the final expression for marginal congestion costs in p.c.u. hours: $t(1/2 - O/2C + O/U)$.

This formula is what is now used, albeit in a slightly different form, by the Ministry of Transport as a first step in assessing marginal congestion costs. Its application to a particular traffic flow through a particular intersection clearly requires the measurement of t, C, O and U. Except for C this is not easy; O is the excess over C of the rate of arrival of vehicles at the back of the queue and t is the period over which this arrival rate is maintained. But the position of the back of the queue varies and is often not sharply defined, making observation difficult. Nor is it easy to decide just when the flow drops from an average value of $C + O$ to one of $C - U$. The application of the formula by the Ministry has avoided these problems, however, by using rough and ready figures for an average intersection. For example, the estimates currently used for the central area are:

t assumed to be $1\frac{1}{2}$ hours,
C set at 2,500 p.c.u.s per hour,
O assumed to be 10 per cent of C for a half-hour high peak and

3 per cent for half an hour on either side, averaging 5·33 per cent,

U derived by assuming $C - U$ to be $2/3$ of $C + U$.

The extra annual delay caused by extra vehicle trips is then obtained for central roads by multiplying up the results given by the formula for one intersection by:

Miles of roads		*Intersections*		*No. of peaks*
affected	×	*per mile*	×	*per year*
(100)		(1)		(500)

While this sort of application of the formula is useful for rough and ready global calculations, there is a need for simpler but more accurate methods which could be applied to particular routes. In the sort of case where a change impinges not upon London in general but upon particular parts of it this need is obvious.

One such method is suggested by some recent work on airport congestion.[9] A *typical* extra vehicle on average holds up each subsequent arrival by $1/C$ (the time taken, on average, for one vehicle to cross the intersection) until the queue has dissipated. Suppose that after the extra vehicle gets to the head of the queue another N vehicles cross before the queue has disappeared H hours later. Since N vehicles take H hours, the time for one vehicle (i.e. $1/C$) is H/N. Multiplying this by the number of vehicles held up gives the astonishingly simple answer for total delay to others at the intersection of: $(H/N)N = H$.

Thus if an extra typical vehicle arrives at the back of the queue at 8.10, crossing the intersection at 8.15, and if the queue lasts till 9.30, the extra delay imposed on other vehicles is simply one and a quarter vehicle hours. If the additional vehicle is not typical of the vehicles in the queue the time must be multiplied by p/pi, where p = number of passenger car units represented by the additional vehicle and pi = average number of passenger car units per vehicle in the queue.

An estimate of the marginal congestion caused by an extra vehicle can thus be made by noting the time it crossed the intersection and the time the queue ends. This can be done for a whole series of intersections traversed by a vehicle so that marginal congestion can be estimated for a whole route.

This simple answer can be shown to be the same as that contained

---

[9] Referred to in Chapter 5, footnote 2, p. 48 above.

in the formula considered above for the case when the extra vehicle joins the queue just half-way through the period lasting t hours. At this point of time there are $Ot/2$ vehicles already in the queue moving at a rate of $1/C$ so that the extra vehicle will get across the intersection $Ot/2C$ hours after joining, i.e. $t/2 + Ot/2C$ hours after the queue started. Subtracting this from the whole time the queue persists gives the remaining duration of the queue

$$H = \left(t + \frac{Ot}{U}\right) - \left(\frac{t}{2} + \frac{Ot}{2C}\right)$$

which reduces to:

$$t\left(\frac{1}{2} - \frac{O}{2C} + \frac{O}{U}\right).$$

There thus appears to be no need to measure t, C, O or U as the Ministry's method suggests. H can be measured directly and more accurately.

9

AN ISLAND SHIPPING SERVICE

This chapter, unlike the rest, is about a private enterprise, not a public one. It is nevertheless included because the principles which it applies are no different from those relevant to public enterprises.

The North of Scotland, Orkney and Shetland Shipping Company Limited (known as the 'North Company') operates scheduled shipping services between the mainland of Scotland and the Orkney and Shetland Islands. In 1968 fares and freight charges had to be increased. This raised the issue of whether their structure as well as their level needed alteration, and the following suggestions were put forward.[1]

There are two features of the present structure which strike us as economically inefficient in the sense that they involve an absence of incentive to use the carrying capacity provided by the shipping service as fully as possible. The first feature is that the pattern of charges for different kinds of freight is not related to the pattern of costs. These costs broadly consist of two main elements: loading and unloading on the one hand and the provision of cubic feet of freight space between the port of origin and that of destination on the other. This latter element must clearly be uniform as between different kinds of freight since the available space can be used for all of them. Yet the freight charges do not reflect this uniformity. Examples of rates from Kirkwall to Leith and from Aberdeen to Lerwick for a few major items are shown below. Estimated loading and unloading costs have been deducted and the balance expressed in pence per cubic foot of shipping space required for each item.

The divergences are wide. The reason for their existence seems to

[1] The rest of this chapter reproduces the bulk of Chapter 5 of *Passenger Fares and Freight Charges of the North of Scotland, Orkney and Shetland Shipping Company Limited*, Report 67 of The National Board for Prices and Incomes (HMSO Cmnd. 3631, May 1968); reproduced with the permission of the Controller of Her Majesty's Stationery Office. The proposals made were not accepted, unfortunately.

CALCULATED SHIPMENT CHARGES IN PENCE PER CUBIC
FOOT OF FREIGHT SPACE

Kirkwall to Leith		Aberdeen to Lerwick	
Eggs	10·5	Feeding stuffs	4·5
Store cattle	5·0	Manures	6·0
Sheep	4·6	Flour	4·3
Spirits	7·0	Lard	12·3
		Spirits	27·5
		Sugar	12·3
		Vegetables	10·2
		Accompanied cars:	
		Single journey	5·7
		Half three-month return	2·9

be that when freight charges have had to be increased in the past,
commercial considerations and a concern for the impact upon the
island economies have combined to induce the North Company to
concentrate the increases upon those items least likely to be adversely
affected. While this is understandable, the resulting cross-subsidiza-
tion of some items by others cannot but have adverse long-run
effects upon the pattern of economic activity in the islands. The cross-
subsidies mean that the relative costs to the islanders of various
activities which are significantly affected by freight charges fail to
reflect the relative real costs. Thus decisions which are sensible from
the point of view of the individuals concerned may not be so from an
overall point of view. The adaptation of the structure of economic
activity to changes in relative costs and prices may therefore be
impeded.

The remedy is clear. By and large, the structure of freight charges
should reflect loading and unloading costs together with the amount
of cargo space required. Since the present structure can be said to
involve a considerable element of 'what the traffic will bear', it
follows that a changeover to the type of structure proposed here
would, taken by itself, produce either a loss of revenue or a loss of
traffic. To avoid the latter the former must be accepted.

The second feature of the present structure, which applies to
passengers as well as freight, is its failure to reflect the seasonal and
directional pattern of costs. There is, on all routes, a great deal of
spare passenger capacity outside the tourist season. For most of the
year there is a great deal of spare freight capacity on the southbound
routes, and also throughout the year on the northbound routes

generally. Given a regular service, the extra costs that would be incurred by using some of this empty space are, in the case of freight, more or less limited to the loading and unloading costs of any additional freight carried. Similarly, the extra costs of carrying additional passengers outside the summer season are very small. Yet in both cases the charges levied by the North Company very substantially exceed these costs. Thus additional traffic which might usefully be carried is discouraged. Furthermore, there is no pecuniary incentive for those shippers who could avoid sending freight in the peak periods to do so.

The importance of the seasonal excess capacity is shown by expressing average directional demand in the off-peak periods as percentages of the demand at the greater of the peaks irrespective of direction (at present the greater of the peaks are all on southbound routes). These percentages are given in the accompanying table for the company's major routes.

What is required to stimulate greater use of the excess capacity is a lower level of fares and charges at times and in directions when utilization of capacity is low. The principle which we suggest is that, in the busy months, charges and fares should be as high as is consistent with a high degree of capacity utilization; this is achieved by the present levels of charges which are based on what the 'traffic will bear'. Higher charges would create under-utilization while lower charges would encourage a greater flow of traffic than can be provided for by the present service. Neither is desirable, since the former would be wasteful while the latter would require space to be allocated arbitrarily.

Leaving aside passenger fares, to which we return later, freight charges should be notably lower during those periods when capacity utilization is low. With present flows, this would result in low charges in both directions outside the summer peak on the Pentland Firth crossing, and low charges for other northbound traffic throughout the year and for other southbound traffic for the greater part of the year. The principle which should obtain for freight charges is that they should always be at least sufficient to cover loading and unloading costs. Furthermore, they should only substantially exceed these amounts to avoid the generation of new peaks in traffic. Thus freight charges for both slack and busy months, and passenger fares for the busy months, would be set having regard to their effect on the volume of traffic. This, however, is already involved in so far as

PEAK AND 'OFF-PEAK' DEMAND[1]

Route	Peak Periods	Average demand in 'off peak' periods as a percentage of southbound peak levels	
		North	South
Orkney–Mainland (Pentland Firth)			
Passengers	July 16th–September 9th	12	12
Freight[2,3]	July 16th–September 9th	22	14
Orkney–Mainland (Other)			
Passengers	July 16th–September 9th	12½	16
Freight[2]	October 8th–December 2nd	37	28
Shetland–Mainland			
Passengers	July 16th–September 9th	16½	14½
Freight[2]	September 10th–November 4th	34	19

[1] Traffic has been analysed in thirteen four-weekly periods. The Lerwick-North Isles of Shetland service is excluded.

[2] Freight demands have been calculated in terms of cubic feet using different 'stowability' factors for each type of freight.

[3] The bulk of the Pentland Firth freight peak is caused by accompanied cars, so that it necessarily coincides with the passenger peak, in contrast with other routes.

'what the traffic will bear' has played a part. The new element, therefore, is that encouraging traffic rather than maintaining revenue takes over as the primary criterion.

Like the change in the structure of fares and freight charges proposed above, the introduction of a seasonal and directional element would involve a loss of revenue. Yet a net increase is required. The solution we propose involves contracts made between the Orkney and Zetland County Councils on the one hand and the North Company on the other. These contracts would provide for payment by the County Councils of that part of the North Company's estimated costs not expected to be recovered by fares and charges fixed according to the principles outlined. These costs, and the revenue from fares and charges, would naturally depend upon the nature of the service provided and this would be specified in the contracts.

It is an essential feature of the scheme that the substantial contribution resulting from the proposed contracts should be financed by the islands' ratepayers. The consequential increase in local rates coupled with the new charges structure would alter the way in which the islanders paid the North Company for their shipping services. The scheme would thus involve a mixture of collective and individual payments to replace the present system of exclusively individual payments by passengers and shippers of freight. The justification for this is that the shipping service does have some of the features of communal services such as, to name but two examples, road maintenance and refuse collection, which are provided by a single organization and paid for by ratepayers. In view of their relative isolation, the provision of a regular shipping service has a utility and convenience to the islanders which is not adequately measured by the actual use which they and their suppliers make of it. There is thus a strong case for the islanders to act together, through their own elected local authorities, in determining the nature and cost of their shipping services. Since the independent fiscal resources of the County Councils are limited to local rates, there is no option but to use the rating system for this purpose.

In that increased local rates make up for reduced charges under our proposals, and hence for the loss of revenue to the North Company, the *total* amount paid by the islanders would be unchanged. But the better use of the carrying capacity provided by the shipping services would clearly benefit the islanders as a whole. Thus, on balance, the removal of the economic inefficiencies resulting from the present charges structure would improve the overall economic position of the islands. The incidence of the change on individuals, on the other hand, is impossible to assess since the prosperity of many islanders not only depends directly on the shipping charges they pay but also on the prosperity of their customers and suppliers in the islands. But given an overall improvement, few ratepayers could convincingly argue that the scheme would damage their interests.

Since local authority responsibility and local rates finance are an essential part of the scheme we propose, and because the bulk of passenger traffic consists of visitors who are not ratepayers, passenger fares have to be treated rather differently from freight charges. An increase over the present level of fares is appropriate for the busy season, as some increase can probably be secured without sensibly reducing the level of summer tourist traffic. However, a reduction in passenger fares below present levels in the slack season would be unwarranted, since any revenue loss would be borne by islanders – most of whom are not passengers – through corresponding increases either in freight rates under present arrangements or in payments made as ratepayers under our proposals.

Choices that are made in the next few years, particularly those which will arise when ships have to be replaced, are vital to the social and economic future of the islands. It is therefore desirable that the islanders, who will have to help to pay the piper, should also help to call the tune – that is, to have a say in the choices involved. Even on the narrowest economic grounds, investment decisions respecting island enterprises need to be co-ordinated with the North Company's investment decisions which will determine the kind of shipping service provided in the future. There is at present no effective means whereby this co-ordination could be achieved. It is therefore an important feature of the scheme which we propose that it provides these means. The negotiations between the two County Councils and the North Company, leading up to the contracts would serve as a planning instrument integrating the islands' agricultural and industrial development with that of transport between the Scottish mainland and the islands.

We have outlined the principles and arguments underlying our proposals for the financing of the islands' shipping services. We now turn in more detail to the main features we would expect to see embodied in any contract which puts the proposals into effect. But first we should make it clear that we do not envisage that a group of councillors would carry out the actual negotiations. In a project of this size the County Councils would be well advised to instruct an independent shipping consultant, totally unconnected with the North Company, to act on their joint behalf. Thus, while the negotiations would take place between the parties directly concerned, they would be conducted by shipping experts.

We would envisage two types of contract. The first type, related to the medium term, would be based on the ships and terminal facilities actually available. It would make provision for the fare structure, the frequency of service and the sums to be paid by the County Councils to the North Company. The second type of contract would provide the framework within which further medium-term contracts would be negotiated, but on the basis of the new ships and terminal facilities that are considered the most economic for the next generation of ships. For the North Company, its main function would be to guarantee further medium-term contracts which would recoup the full capital costs of the new fleet over their expected lives. To the islands, it would guarantee an adequate transport service for the same period between specified ports.

In the longer term, when ships have to be replaced, or when plans to build new terminal facilities have to be put into effect – involving the company in greater depreciation costs and interest charges – the County Councils would be faced with the need to find even more substantial sums of money than those required to implement the initial stages of our proposals. This would entail increased rate payments by the islanders to their shipping services.

The medium-term contracts would provide for a tariff structure but with suitable cost-escalation clauses where necessary. In setting tariff levels we have already suggested the separate criteria for determining the level of passenger fares and freight charges. With regard to passenger fares, we indicated that these should be determined by the principle of 'what the traffic would bear' in the peak. For example, we would expect the first contract to specify passenger fares during the peak holiday period from May to September at levels at least as great as the present levels plus the proposed increase. In the off-peak season, we would expect a lower level of rates.

Freight charges specified in the contracts for each route should also differentiate between peak and off-peak periods and, as these may occur at different times of the year, there may be, at any one time, differences in freight charges for northbound and southbound traffic. We suggest that the level of charges at the peak period should approximate to existing levels after adjustment to bring them to a common rate per cubic foot plus loading and discharging costs. Consideration will have to be given to the need for varying the peak period or for providing modified peakcharges in periods either side of the peak. During the remainder of the year the freight charges should be at a level which approximates to the loading and discharging costs for each category of traffic. We recognize that it may be desirable to move towards this new structure in stages. Certain types of freight, such as cars, may require special treatment.

We asked a number of representative bodies in the islands to comment on the reference and received their views both in writing and orally. Their replies were unanimous in asserting a need for a subsidy which would arrest or even reverse the upward spiral of freight charges and passenger fares which the islands have been experiencing. Some of them asked us to recommend such a subsidy. This, however, seems to us to require a social and political judgement and to extend well beyond the bounds of prices and incomes policy. We cannot therefore make any such recommendation. We wish to make it clear, however, that neither are we recommending against the institution of a subsidy. We therefore confine ourselves to the recommendation that the Government make a firm decision one way or the other as soon as possible.

10

COST ANALYSIS OF NATURAL GAS SUPPLY[1]

Marginal cost in the supply of gas to consumers is not a simple concept and requires a fairly lengthy explanation.

An increment or decrement in the supply of gas should be represented by the change in the consumption of an existing consumer, or by the total consumption of a single new consumer. This means that the increment or decrement is extremely small in relation to total supply – hence the term marginal. Clearly such an increment or decrement has several dimensions, such as its magnitude at different times of the year and whether or not the consumer is already connected to the mains. Its effect on costs will depend on all these things, which is why it is necessary to speak of marginal costs rather than simply of marginal cost. For example, the following marginal costs can be distinguished:

(*a*) The cost of connecting and servicing an additional customer (if the number of therms supplied in each period remains constant);

(*b*) The cost of supplying an additional therm at a particular time off-peak (if the number of therms supplied at other times and the number of customers remain constant);

(*c*) The cost of supplying an additional therm at the peak (if the total therms supplied in each period off-peak and the number of customers remain constant).

Since marginal costs are relevant to tariffs and published tariffs have to be uniform within zones, these costs can usefully be assessed so as to average out differences between consumers within each zone, except when a special agreement with a particular large consumer is under consideration.

The addition to cost resulting from an increment of demand will

---

[1] Appendix D of *Gas Prices* (*Second Report*), Report 102 of The National Board for Prices and Incomes (HMSO Cmnd. 3924, February 1969); reproduced with the permission of the Controller of Her Majesty's Stationery Office.

also depend upon its temperature sensitivity. Neglecting this complication for the moment, however, the important point just made is that marginal costs depend upon the time-pattern of an increment in demand. But this does not mean that a separate analysis has to be made for each conceivable pattern. In the case of the small increments and decrements which are involved, marginal cost is additive so that, for example, the marginal cost of a therm per day in every day of the year is the sum of the marginal costs of a therm per day for the three summer months and for the nine other months. Thus, the structure of marginal costs can be set out by dividing the year into periods and establishing the marginal cost of a therm per day (or whatever unit is chosen) for each of those periods. The number of periods used will vary with the accuracy and complexity of the analysis, which is desirable or achievable. (Allowance for temperature sensitivity, which affects plant mix, also makes for complexity.) Any increment or decrement then has to be described in terms of its size in each of the periods into which the year is divided. Once this is done its marginal costs over the year as a whole can be readily calculated.

Some of the industry's costs derive from connecting customers to the system, reading meters each quarter, attending to complaints, converting appliances, making out bills and rendering accounts. Others derive from the sale of appliances and from overheads. All these are relatively minor and present no analytical problems. This analysis of the structure of natural gas costs can therefore concentrate on transmission, storage, distribution and purchasing costs.

Gas may be supplied direct or from storage. The direct supply will come mostly from the North Sea, though it may be cheaper to provide some peak[2] requirements by importing methane or by

---

[2] Present sales of gas are mostly sensitive to temperature and, in consequence, peak demand occurs in winter. So long as pipes, storage facilities, etc., are sized to meet winter demand, the cost of installing these facilities does not enter into the marginal costs of an increment in summer demand. This could enable the industry to sell natural gas very cheaply at some times of the year. It is, therefore, conceivable that such a big market in interruptible industrial loads could develop that the industry might in time come to supply a demand that was plateau shaped and no longer peaked in the winter. If this were to happen, the capacity of the pipeline and gas wells would be fully used to supply consumers during the daytime for long periods in the year, probably making it unnecessary to provide seasonal storage of LNG except for meeting breakdowns. This would change the cost structure. Meanwhile, however, the industry is currently considering the installation of LNG storage in anticipation of a continuing winter peak. This analysis of the cost structure therefore does the same.

manufacturing SNG. The choice of stores will depend on how often each store is used; some stores will be emptied and refilled only once a year and others more frequently. For stores which are to be frequently filled and emptied it is economic to incur relatively higher capital costs in order to achieve lower running costs. In so far as capital costs are related to the volume of storage capacity, they can be reduced by storing gas in liquefied form so that the holder in which the gas is stored is relatively small. A further economy of capital can be achieved by storing imported liquefied methane rather than incurring the cost of a plant with which to liquefy gas from the bulk transmission system.

In operating the system the various sources of gas will be drawn upon in increasing order of their operating costs subject to the constraint that stored reserves of gas needed for meeting peak demands are not prematurely run down. When drawing on plants in order of their operating costs an increment of demand at any time will be met from a source which is more expensive to run than the sources which are operating at full capacity. Thus, the cost per therm of increments of demand will vary from period to period and from place to place according to the level of demand. When, as is likely, in the early winter months the order of taking gas is constrained because a store could not be refilled in time to meet the expected demand arising later in the year, a more expensive source may be used in preference to the cheaper apparently available source. As before, the incremental costs of supply will be determined by whichever source is chosen. Increments of demand close to the peak are likely to cause a need for the system to add to its capacity to supply gas in the winter months. The cheapest way to meet such increment when off-peak gas is available is to increase the amount of storage in the system and to raise the volume of gas available in the store. In this case the costs of extending the amount of storage and putting more gas in store off-peak must be summed to arrive at marginal cost. A third item, the cost of extending the system's delivery capacity, will be added for an increment of demand at peak. This third item consists of an increase in storage delivery capacity (plus reinforcement of the distribution network, which is discussed below). These items and their interrelationships are further examined below, where additional complications are introduced into the analysis.

It is tempting to analyse the cost structure by dividing the accounting cost figures into such categories as capacity-related costs, commodity costs, consumer-related costs and so on and then to divide the total figure for each category by the appropriate denominator to obtain a set of unit cost estimates. Unfortunately, the results of such an approach can diverge widely from the real structure of marginal costs. The reasons for a such a divergence are several. First, the accounting approach assumes proportionality in each cost category, thus equating marginal and average cost by assumption. Second, it is not always clear in advance exactly what categories are appropriate. For example, while it may be obvious that summer and winter should be analysed separately, the length of the winter and summer periods requires investigation. Third, arbitrary allocation of joint cost items is involved. Fourth, it is the future cost of additional assets that is relevant, not the historical cost of existing assets.

To estimate the structure of marginal costs is to describe the cost consequences of alternative future actions. Corresponding to any set of outputs over time, there will be a time-stream of expenditure on providing, maintaining and running the system. To ascertain the marginal cost of any specified increment (or decrement) of gas supply, two alternative time-streams of future expenditures of providing slightly different outputs, must be compared. To carry out such a comparison the industry would first need to forecast demand for a number of years ahead and then, using its planning models, calculate the least-cost method of deploying new and existing resources to meet this demand subject to statutory, financial, contractual and other constraints. Investment and operating plans will be based on forecast demand, but if an increment or decrement of demand occurs, an adjustment will be necessary. Another calculation will therefore be necessary using planning models to derive the minimum cost of the adjusted system. (In this second calculation it may have to be assumed that some of the investment required to meet the forecast demand has already been committed.) The difference between the two (minimum) system costs would be the marginal cost of meeting the increment or decrement. Thus, the calculations which derive marginal costs are similar to those required to decide how to meet future demand at minimum cost.

The approach just outlined needs to be supplemented because the models on which it is based do not extend to the whole of the distribution system. They do not and could not easily be made to cover the whole network of low-pressure pipelines and for this part of the system other methods will have to be used. The costs to be analysed in other ways are the marginal costs of connection and of low- and medium-pressure reinforcement. In each case, it is necessary to rely on the cost calculations of the distribution engineers aided by network analysis. As always the minimum incremental costs of meeting a permanent new load are required. Thus, it is important for this purpose as well as for correct investment decisions that the engineers' costings should be based, wherever possible, on projects which are not just feasible but which minimize the future cost of supply.

The distribution costs of connecting each new consumer are estimated by the engineering department at the time when the proposal to connect him is appraised. In the case of a new housing estate, these costs would normally be meters, services and estate mains and governors. All these costs ought to be readily available. But greater difficulty arises in the case of reinforcement.

Both the connection of new consumers and increases in the gas consumption of existing consumers bring forward the time when the distribution system upstream will require reinforcement. It would be impractical to try to estimate case by case the present worth of the costs to be incurred in the future, because the time of these reinforcements was brought forward. It will be sufficient if marginal cost relates to the average of the reinforcement costs caused by the supply of additional peak day therms at a large number of different locations within a zone.

Supplying additional peak day therms at a large number of different locations requires the timing of a large number of reinforcement sequences to be brought forward and the result is to add a permanent increment to the distribution capacity of the whole system. If the present worth of the costs of creating and maintaining this total increment in distribution capacity is divided by the number of additional peak day therms which it is installed to provide, then an estimate of the marginal cost of distribution per peak day therm of capacity is obtained. This must be grossed up to allow for the normal excess of capacity over peak day demand to obtain marginal cost per peak day therm of demand. Since an increase in demand leads to a chain reaction of reinforcement starting near the consumer and finishing at the gas source, it may simplify matters to estimate the reinforcement costs of the medium- and low-pressure systems separately. Therefore, it would be necessary to collect data from a large number of medium- and low-pressure reinforcement schemes and, taking each pressure level separately, to divide the capital cost by the number of additional peak day therms which were thus provided. In this way, the average capital cost per additional peak day therm of reinforcing the medium- and low-pressure distribution system could be estimated. To this would have to be added the cost per peak day therm of maintaining that capacity, assuming that assets are renewed as they wear out.

In the following paragraphs some aspects of the least-cost solution to the problem of transmitting natural gas from the beach-head (and from Canvey Island) and either delivering it directly into low-pressure systems for distribution or first storing it and then delivering it are examined in more detail. The purpose is to show how the character-istics of the system are reflected in the structure of its marginal costs and to throw some light on certain problems of optimization. This aim is qualitative and an analytical approach is therefore called for. A model designed to give working numerical answers would have to be formulated in programming terms and would therefore give less insight into the nature of a few key relationships. For present purposes, the analytical approach is therefore preferable, particularly since it admits the possibility of a number of first-stage simplifying assumptions, which enable these key relationships to stand out clearly. The analysis, which is referred to in the main part of the report as a guideline model, is tentative and is presented in outline merely as a suggestion of the sort of approach which usefully illuminates some central problems.

System costs, including the beach-head cost of natural gas, obviously depend upon the level and nature of the demand for gas, which it is planned to meet. With tariffs reflecting marginal cost and affecting the level and nature of demand there is consequently a feed-back at work. The demand side of the analysis is not taken up here, however, and the future evolution of demand is assumed to be known and given.

As explained earlier the least-cost solution requires pipeline deli-very capacity after the first few years to be less than the maximum demand to be met, the difference being made up by delivery from storage. The pipeline network will thus have a higher load factor than final demand, some of the gas taken through the pipeline being put into storage at night and in the summer in order to help meet demand peaks during the day and in winter. It is also possible that

SNG will be produced and liquefied petroleum gas supplied in order to help meet demand at peak periods.

These various ways of meeting demand exhibit different cost relationships. To see this consider first the beach-head price of natural gas itself. This price is not just so many pence a therm. The form of contract provides that the Gas Council makes a fixed annual payment for the right to take a specified annual volume of gas without at any time exceeding a specified maximum rate of flow. The contracts generally oblige producers to have available 167 per cent of the average daily quantity during the winter giving a 60 per cent daily load factor if the specified annual volume is taken. A complication which is neglected in what follows for expository reasons is that there is not a single maximum rate of flow for the whole year but a monthly series which is lower in the summer months to allow for maintenance of the production facilities. Extra gas in excess of the specified annual volume, but within the specified maximum rate, costs a lower ('valley gas') price. Extra gas above the specified maxima would presumably require revised or additional contracts involving an increased fixed annual sum. These however would also raise the annual entitlement thus reducing 'valley gas' purchases as a partial offset (unless annual volume rose *pro rata* at the same time).

The incremental delivery capacity cost of direct supply from the North Sea (including the cost of the pipeline and compressors as well as that of the gas) would be higher than that of any alternative if it caused the specified maxima to be exceeded. If the specified maxima were not exceeded then the cost of the gas would be lower. However, both in this and the previous case once additional delivery capacity has been provided to meet an increase in the peak, the costs of raising off-peak supply would be low (they would chiefly consist in the running of compressors and perhaps the purchase of 'valley gas'). The costs of increasing supply from storage off-peak would be higher than this since they would include not only the costs of purchasing and transmitting the gas but also the costs of running the store. This latter is negligible in the case of most diurnal stores, but it is significant for aquifers and higher still for LNG. Although liquid gas is much denser than compressed gas and its cost per unit of storage volume is therefore low, there are extra costs of liquefying the gas and keeping it liquid. The capital and running costs of the liquefaction plant are largely determined by the rate at which gas has to be put into store. As regards the cost of increasing storage delivery capacity as a means of meeting an increase in peak demand, the relevant cost is high in the case of aquifers (but below that of direct supply from the North Sea). The cost of adding to the delivery capacity of diurnal and LNG storage is lower but in the case of such stores (unlike aquifers) the costs of adding to storage volume are considerable. Costs are thus not just a simple function of delivery capacity and of throughput; according to the kinds of storage used, they may also be determined by storage inlet capacity, storage volume and storage duration.

It is the interplay of all these cost factors which determines the optimal development of the system through time to meet the development of demand through time. Since, in the present expository context, the latter is taken as given, the optimal development of the system is that which minimizes the present worth of its costs. This minimization is, of course, subject to other constraints in addition to that of meeting demand and two of them appear to be of major importance. First, the volume of gas delivered from store at peak times cannot exceed the volume of gas which can be put into the store by using the pipeline off-peak. Second, the form of contract with the oil companies can mean that the annual volume of gas which can be taken before extra therms cost the 'valley' price is determined by the maximum rate of take contracted for (given the load factor in the contracts).

The interplay of the cost factors described and the influences of the constraints can best be considered by abstracting from demand growth and indivisibility in plant and by examining a single pipeline rather than a network. In these circumstances, with an annual movement of therms per day delivered to the low-pressure system as shown by the continuous curve in the accompanying diagram

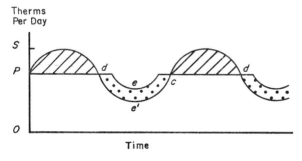

with only one means of storage in use, a maximum daily demand of *OS* could be met by a pipeline capacity of *OP*, a storage inlet capacity of *ee'*, and a storage delivery capacity of *PS*. Off-peak, a volume of gas represented by the dotted area would be put into storage each year. This, less the amount used by the storage plant, equals the cross-hatched area each year which is the portion of demand met from storage. Thus, the use of the pipeline is shown by the line *Pdecd*.

The demand constraint would continue to be satisfied if *OP* were a little smaller and *PS* a little larger and *vice versa*. There are, that is to say, alternative feasible mixes of pipeline and storage. The optimal one, by definition is that where no feasible change would lower costs. At the limit, this requires that the extra capital and running costs of extra pipeline capacity would just be matched by the savings in respect of storage and *vice versa*. Itemizing these gives the following equality, where capital costs are measured as equivalent annuities in order to express all costs in annual terms:

> *marginal pipeline capital costs*
> + *change in pipeline running costs*
> + *marginal annual payment under contract*
> − *saving (if any) on 'valley gas' purchase*
> = *marginal storage delivery and inlet capital costs*
> + *marginal storage volume capital costs*
> + *change in storage running costs.*

The precise mix where this equality is just satisfied (assuming, for the next few paragraphs, that such a mix exists) clearly depends both on the pattern of demand and on the way in which all the items in the equality vary with capacity and use. Thus the proportion of total capacity provided by storage will be lower, *ceteris paribus*:

—the greater are marginal storage delivery and inlet capital costs in relation to marginal pipeline capital costs and similarly with respect to running costs;
—the greater are marginal storage volume capital costs;
—the smaller is the seasonal swing in demand, because this directly determines the maximum feasible use of storage.

It will be seen that the form of contract with the oil companies assumed above introduces a significant discontinuity, described above as a constraint. So long as the load factor at the beach-head falls short of the 60 per cent implicit in the contract, the marginal cost to the Gas Council of extra therms is zero[3] except when they involve an increase in the maximum rate of take and a consequent increase in annual payment under a revised or new contract. If, on the other hand, load factor at the beach-head exceeded 60 per cent, the marginal cost of extra therms would be greater, equalling the 'valley gas' price plus other running costs, except possibly when demand involves an increase in the maximum rate of take. The reason is that such an increase might mean an increased annual contract payment, which would presumably be partly offset by a reduction in 'valley gas' purchases.

Each side of the equality measures the system cost of achieving a small increment of delivery capacity, since the absence of inequality means that there is no gain to be had from substituting output achieved by one form of delivery capacity for another and making the necessary appropriate change in storage volume capacity. Similar equalities for any other pair of kinds of peak capacity are conditions of an optimum, which is unconstrained with respect to storage, so that the analysis has greater generality than its exposition, as if there were only one form of storage, might suggest. But the important point is that these are all equalities and each side of all of them measures the system cost of achieving a small increment of delivery capacity. This common value is nothing but the marginal cost of meeting an increase in demand at peak. Hence no matter what form of additional delivery capacity is installed, its cost can be represented, as above, as the cost of providing gas from storage.

At times when demand is lower but still higher than the capacity of the pipeline – that is, in the region *PS* in the diagram – marginal cost will include no delivery capacity cost but may still include other capital costs. Thus, in terms of the diagram, where only one form of storage is assumed to be used in order to meet demand in excess of *OP*, a demand increment could be shown as an upward bulge not affecting the summit of the curve above *cd*. The resulting increase in the cross-hatched area requires a corresponding increase in the dotted area, that is, an upward shift of *dec*. It is clear that this will involve not only greater storage running costs but also the costs of

---

[3] Or the present worth of their future value if taken in later years, since under the contracts gas paid for, but not taken in any year, may be taken free of charge during the next several years after the specified annual volumes for these years have been taken.

extending both storage inlet capacity and storage volume capacity. Extending the analysis, there will be as many different demand ranges within *PS*, each with its own marginal cost, as there are types of plant (storage, SNG, etc.) used in the system.

Finally, at times when demand is lower along the segments *dec* of the curve in the diagram, an increment of demand can be met by pumping more gas along the pipeline. Marginal running cost (including, if operative, the 'valley gas' price) plus the cost of increasing storage inlet capacity then constitutes the marginal cost. The last item comes in when the increment in demand results in an increase in the maximum daily rate at which storage has to be filled, *ee'*.

The structure of marginal costs is thus seen to be essentially related to the mix of plant chosen to meet the demand so that cost analysis is part of the analysis of the optimum mix.

So far it has been assumed that the storage constraint is ineffective. It may be, however, that the equality mentioned above cannot be met because storage is so cheap relative to pipeline costs (as it might be if suitable large aquifers were found), that the mix which minimized capacity cost is rendered impossible, requiring more gas to be put into storage than is available off-peak. In such a case the situation will be as shown in the second diagram. Under these conditions the pipeline is used at 100 per cent load factor and *any* increment in demand, regardless of when it occurs, necessitates an increase in pipeline capacity. But it will never pay to meet an increment solely by increasing pipeline delivery capacity (except in the limiting case where the load factor of the increment is 100 per cent), since the situation where the storage constraint is effective arises where the equality mentioned above is not fulfilled and where incremental storage, if feasible, would thus be cheaper. Hence, the cheapest way of meeting any increment of demand under such circumstances is to increase pipeline capacity so as to preserve operation at 100 per cent load factor. This means raising the annual volume of pipeline throughput by the annual volume of the demand increment and altering storage sufficiently to, so to speak, 'convert' this flat increment of pipeline throughput into the time-shape of the demand increment.

Consider first an increment in peak demand. This will require both an increase in storage delivery capacity and in storage volume capacity. Second, an increment when demand is between *P* and *S* will require only the latter and thus has a lower marginal cost.

Finally, an increment in demand at times when demand is less than *OP* will actually reduce required storage volume and delivery capacity. (It may, or may not, reduce storage inlet capacity). Hence the marginal cost of meeting such an increment in demand is net of the saving in storage costs. In all three cases, marginal cost will, of course, also include the increase in annual contract payment, increased 'valley gas' purchases and the costs of adding pipeline

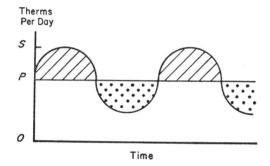

capacity. As in the unconstrained case, there are seen to be three levels of marginal cost according to the timing of the increment of demand and there would be more levels than this if there were more than one kind of storage or if SNG were produced to help meet peak demand.

The analysis presented is so obviously simplified that it is unnecessary to recite all the complications which it leaves out. But despite this, as will now be argued, it has value in showing the sort of relationships which exist in reality and which need to be understood in order that the particular numerical results generated by a full-scale programming calculation can be interpreted. Such a calculation can deal with the complications left out here, but yields results which are not easy to understand without the aid of an analytical approach.

While a full-scale programming calculation would naturally relate to the minimum cost of meeting a demand, which is growing through time where pipeline and storage capacity can be increased only be discrete amounts, the analysis so far relates to a steady-state solution where pipeline and storage capacity are divisible. It therefore illuminates the nature of cost structure, only if the desirable effect of these assumptions in achieving simplification is not bought at the cost of distortion. Thus, the question is whether results which, though much more complex, are similar in principle flow from a multi-year analysis which takes account of indivisibility. The answer is that they do. The marginal cost of an increment or decrement of supply during any specified period of any year is the dual of the demand constraint for that period in the programming calculation. This is as true when the calculation relates to demand changing from year to year, with integer restrictions on plant provision, as it is for the simpler calculation relating to a steady state year after year with no such restrictions.

The new complexity means that minimum cost now relates to the time path of outlays on providing and operating plant and purchasing gas, given the time path of demand. Once again, it is a condition of the optimal solution that no feasible substitution of pipeline delivery capacity for storage capacity or of one type of storage for another reduces the present worth of system costs. Such a substitution can now relate to timing as well as type of capacity, however, or to both together. An example would be an increase in the size of pipeline provided in one year and a postponement of the addition of storage to the system. Thus, the number of possible types of substitution is multiplied as compared with the steady-state case. The non-optimality of any one such substitution can no longer be expressed as simply as in the equality, since the terms there now become the present worth of time-streams rather than just annual amounts. Furthermore, these conditions are now inequalities relating to discrete substitutions (rather than equalities relating to infinitely small substitutions) and the substitutions may alter total capacity. Marginal cost for any given period of the year may, in consequence, be different for an increment and for a decrement and vary sharply from one year to another.

While these complexities in the cost structure may be directly relevant to negotiations with large consumers, they are less relevant to published tariffs for broad consumer classes. Such tariffs should not fluctuate from year to year and therefore need to reflect the average of marginal costs in a mature system both between load increments and decrements and over a period of years. The end result of the programming calculation of the structure of marginal cost will therefore be simpler than the last paragraph might suggest. What is important is that this structure will have the same characteristics as those adduced above in the analysis of the steady-state case. Marginal cost, that is to say, varies from period to period within the year according to the sources of gas in use and the costs of the cheapest method of increasing delivery capacity. The appropriate division of the year into periods is not determined *a priori* but emerges from the optimization process, given the pattern of demand.

The introduction of uncertainty affects the optimal amount and mix of delivery capacity but does not alter the essential characteristics of marginal costs described above. How incremental demands are actually supplied at any particular time will depend both on the level of demand and on any plant breakdowns which then occur. Uncertainty about them means that only the 'expected' costs of meeting incremental demands can be calculated. 'Expected' costs can be derived as an average of the costs that might be incurred, each weighted by the likelihood of incurring them.

The marginal cost of supplying an increment of demand is likely to be greater in a cold year when the level of demand is higher. If an increment of load is specified in terms of normal temperatures, it is necessary to allow for the fact that at times of low temperature, when marginal costs are higher, any 'temperature sensitive' increment will itself be larger. Thus the 'expected' costs of supplying otherwise similar load increments of different temperature sensitivity will be different. Since space heating shows the highest temperature sensitivity, this aspect of the structure of marginal costs has clear implications for tariff setting.

When incremental costs of supply to a customer are couched in terms of 'expected' costs, the reliability 'component' is inseparable from the normal supply costs. Thus, the introduction of uncertainty is seen to introduce temperature sensitivity and reliability into the analysis, requiring marginal cost to be calculated as an 'expected' variable.

11

INVESTMENT IN GAS DISTRIBUTION[1]

Distribution covers all operations required for the transmission and storage of gas between the gas manufacturing plant or natural gas off-take point and the meter of the final consumer. Thus, investment in distribution includes major schemes for the extension, renewal and reinforcement of mains and storage as well as projects to provide new compressors, governors and other equipment. Many single projects cost over £100,000 and a few cost over £1,000,000. Most investment in distribution is not of this kind, however, but is the sum of many small projects. Each year the West Midlands Board, for example, appraises some 700 new housing estate projects, most of them costing less than £5,000. Minor extensions and reinforcements are also very numerous. The amounts of money which are involved are big enough for it to be important to devise appropriate methods of appraising small projects, although these methods need not necessarily be of the same degree of elaboration as the methods which are used to appraise big projects.

The analysis of distribution projects requires investment appraisal as well as operational research. Individual distribution projects cannot always be incorporated in a plan of the whole system. One reason is that part of the system may have to be planned before the location of the future demand can be forecast in detail. In such cases the plan makes a general provision for distribution and leaves individual distribution projects to be filled in afterwards. When individual distribution projects come to be analysed, such factors as connection costs, appliance installations and the financial contribution which the consumer should make towards the cost will need to be assessed and the techniques of investment appraisal are the most efficient means of doing so.

[1] Appendix C of *Gas Prices* (*Second Report*), Report 102 of the National Board for Prices and Incomes (HMSO Cmnd. 3924, February 1969); reproduced with the permission of the Controller of Her Majesty's Stationery Office. A few passages have been omitted.

Since the industry must estimate its future revenue and expenditure and hence its borrowing requirements year by year, the financial consequences of investment decisions must be examined. In a financial appraisal such items as the cost of borrowing will need to be estimated. This cost may well vary from one source of funds to another. For example, the cost of borrowing from the Exchequer will not necessarily be the same as that of borrowing from other sources. On the other hand, in an economic appraisal using discounted cash flows for planning purposes the operation of the discount factor will implicitly set the cost of all new capital at whatever rate of discount is used. In this way the two forms of appraisal are distinct. They are also distinct to the extent that whereas economic appraisals form part of the long-term planning process and cover fifteen years or more, financial appraisals are relatively short-term and deal with a period only five years ahead. The sum of the industry's financial appraisals constitutes its Capital Development Programme.

A technical appraisal is needed to ensure that the appropriate pressures and flows of gas are provided to each consumer and an economic appraisal is needed to ensure that the investment criteria set out in the White Paper[2] are applied. This distinction between the purposes of a technical and an economic appraisal does not correspond to the distinction between the work of the engineering department and that of the accounting or finance department in appraising a project. If the engineers restricted themselves to a technical appraisal, they would put forward all feasible solutions to the engineering problems which they face. Instead, they put forward only one or a few feasible solutions, having eliminated the rest on grounds of cost. This preliminary selection from the feasible alternatives is essentially an economic function and much of it is carried out at local level. For example, the choice of pipe sizes is an appropriate subject for economic analysis. But no instances were found where it was undertaken by finance departments; it was everywhere carried out by the engineers themselves or by OR scientists. This spread of economic decision taking among departments and between headquarters and local staff is very desirable. But it means that all the staff concerned, not just the accountants, need to be familiar

---

[2] *Nationalized Industries: A review of economic and financial objectives* (HMSO Cmnd. 3437). This laid down 8 per cent as the test discount rate to be used for investment appraisal, a figure subsequently raised to 10 per cent.

with the techniques of economic appraisal and the principles laid down in the White Paper.

The appropriate way to carry out an economic appraisal of most distribution projects is by discounting cash flows (DCF). In some Area Boards this is thought of as an accounting technique and the chief accountant's department is the only department to use it. In these boards the chief accountant's department carries out DCF analysis for other departments on request. The danger of this is that some problems which would be suitable for analysis by DCF may not be recognized as such in other departments. Clearly it is desirable that experience of making DCF calculations should be widespread within each board, if full use is to be made of the technique.

Before DCF began to be used, investment decisions were based on simpler calculations and rules of thumb. For example, the engineers would size their pipes for three or four times the current load and the accountants would require a new housing estate to provide a surplus on revenue account of, say, fourpence per therm of gas supplied. DCF techniques have only recently been brought into use in the industry and their use is more widespread in some boards than in others. However, every board now uses some version of DCF to appraise proposals to connect new customers.

Distribution projects are either to connect new customers or to reinforce the existing pipes and storage. The main features specific to each of these two types of problem will be outlined and then some of the practical issues which arise will be considered.

Where an application for a new supply of gas relates to premises which are within twenty-five yards of an existing main, the Area Board is statutorily obliged to provide the new supply. In other cases, and there are many of them, the Area Board has the option of not providing it. However, no Area Board will refuse to connect a new customer. If the net revenue to be expected from supplying him will not provide a satisfactory return on the minimum investment which would be necessary to connect him, then he will be required to make a financial contribution towards the cost of the connection. The required contribution will be that amount which reduces the Area Board's investment to the level which would be justified by the net revenue from the project. Thus, if their forecasts of costs and revenues are accurate, the Area Boards will always earn the return which they desire on such investment. The main purpose of their economic appraisals of new connections is then to calculate whether a financial contribution is required, and, if so, how much it should be. This way of expressing the objective is satisfactory provided that it is not forgotten that it is the allocation of real resources which is the primary concern. The potential new customer should be given the opportunity to buy gas at a price which is based on the minimum cost to the Area Board of supplying it. The required return on the Area Board's capital is part of this cost; it is a constraint and not an objective.

Having once provided a supply of gas to any premises, the Area Boards are under a statutory obligation to maintain that supply so long and in such quantities as the customer requires it. There are statutory safety limits which must be observed too. Thus, the Area Boards do not normally have the option of not repairing or replacing an existing pipe which has become defective, or of not reinforcing a pipe whose carrying capacity will shortly be overtaken by rising demand. However, if the need for reinforcement is forecast sufficiently early, then the latest date when it would become obligatory may be deferred or brought forward by varying the local selling effort. Let it be supposed that an increase in selling effort would increase appliance sales, the consumption of gas and hence the Area Board's revenue. This extra selling effort would be justified only if the increase which it was expected to achieve in the present worth of revenues exceeded the increase which it was expected to incur in the present worth of system costs, including the cost of bringing forward the date of reinforcement. Calculations such as this may be relevant in cases where an Area Board is considering the reinforcement of a single link main which connects a local area to the rest of the grid. But most reinforcements are not of this kind, and they can be dealt with more simply. The problem in the majority of cases is just to satisfy the statutory constraints at minimum cost.

In some cases the statutory obligation to continue to supply existing customers may oblige the Area Boards to undertake renewal which will not yield an acceptable financial return. Such cases are perhaps especially likely to occur in rural areas where there are social benefits which are not reflected in financial accounts. However, there is no general presumption that as the system is adapted to changed circumstances its profitability will necessarily decline.

The principal choices which have to be made in the case of reinforcement projects can now be enumerated. Since it will often be advantageous to deal with related problems in a single scheme the first choice is the scope of the project. Then there may be choices between temporary and more permanent solutions, immediate and delayed starts, rapid and delayed completions, one size, location or pressure level and another and high- and low-pressure storage and transmission. People with experience in the industry can, and usually do, resolve many of these choices summarily. But there is a need for systematic analysis too. Those who have to make the decisions need to experiment with making formal analyses for those classes of case where the potential benefits seem to be large and compare the costs of making these assessments with the average saving achieved as a result. It should then be possible to draw up working rules for deciding when the matter should be analysed systematically and when it should simply be left to the judgment of experienced people.

The scope for systematic analysis will be illustrated by examining the problem of pipe sizing. This is an important matter for the purchase and laying of pipes is the biggest item of the Area Board's capital expenditure and, therefore, a small improvement in sizing decisions could yield large economies.

The simplest problem of pipe sizing arises where a single pipe connects to the rest of the system a group of customers whose demand for gas is forecast to increase steadily. There are many instances of this, particularly in boards which serve big areas with a dispersed population. The problem for the Area Boards is to decide how many years load growth to anticipate when sizing the single link main. Research is known to have been done on this by two boards, one using numerical examples and the other using differentiation. The optimal period of load growth to size for was put by the two studies at about ten years and at twenty-four to thirty-two years respectively. The optimal period to size for is determined in part by local costs and by the rate of growth of local demand. Thus, the optimal sizing policy will vary to some extent from place to place and from time to time and it is not to be expected that all sizing studies will reach the same conclusion. However, all studies of this kind ought to make the same assumptions concerning inflation. In the present example, the first board ignored inflation whereas the second board built into its cost figures an annual rate of inflation of $2\frac{1}{4}$ per cent. Both used a discount rate of 8 per cent. In appraisals of this kind inflation should be taken into account only to the extent that it affects relative costs. In the present example, it affects equally the costs of the alternative sizing policies which are being compared.

The sizing of high-pressure pipes has to take into account their usefulness for line pack as well as for transmission. The value of line pack is the net saving which it brings about in other transmission and storage costs. A pipe sized for transmission only and without regard to line pack will all the same be capable of being used for line pack in its early years when it has spare capacity. To use this line pack potential may require the incurring of costs such as additional costs of compression. The extra costs, if there are any, together with the cost of the gas packed into the line (which will be cheap off-peak gas), will, in present worth terms, be the cost of gas from line pack storage. This present worth needs to be compared with the present worth of the system costs which would be incurred by alternative ways of meeting the same demand. These are the installation of additional transmission capacity and the provision of various other types and combinations of high and low pressure storage. If line pack is the cheapest alternative, then it should be chosen. Since the capacity of the pipe will be used increasingly for transmission as load grows, it follows that the spare capacity which is available for line pack will gradually fall to zero. However, the value of line pack may be so great as to justify laying a pipe bigger than would be warranted by transmission alone. Instances were found where pipes were sized in this way. Their installation is justified if, and only if, the transmission and storage capacity which they provide cannot be supplied more cheaply by other means.

Medium- and low-pressure pipes cannot provide line pack in significant amounts. However, the fact that they are usually arranged in complicated networks makes for considerable technical and economic difficulties in deciding which size of pipe to lay in any given case. The technical problem is to select and locate the pipes so as to provide adequate pressures and flows of gas to each consumer. The economic problem is to minimize pipe costs subject to these technical constraints. Until recently the economic problem was solved by rule of thumb. But a considerable advance was achieved at the end of 1967 with the construction of a computer model which uses a systematic trial and error procedure to minimize pipe costs for any given load. The model was the work of the North Western Board acting on behalf of a joint working party organized through the Gas Council.

The North Western Board's model takes as its starting point a network in which the layout of pipes and the inflows and outflows of gas are given. Each pipe in the model is given the smallest allowable diameter initially and the model is changed by increasing the diameter of one pipe at a time, the pipe to be altered in each case being the one having the greatest pressure drop per unit of length. The increase in diameter is in each case the minimum which is allowable. The computer proceeds in this way until it satisfies the minimum technical conditions as regards flows and pressures. At this point sizes and hence pipeline costs have been minimized subject to the technical constraints and the problem is solved. The North Western Board reduced its expenditure on pipes by 7 per cent below what they would otherwise have been in cases of this kind by substituting the computer method for the rules of thumb which had been used earlier.

Ideally, one would want a computer programme which took account of load growth as well as allowing for the features which are handled by the North Western Board's model (which assumes no load growth). But for the moment load growth has to be dealt with as a separate problem. One way to tackle it would be to apply the North Western Board's model to the load which was forecast for various future years and from this to derive the present worth of the cost of alternative sizing policies. The optimal policy would be that which minimised this present worth. A simpler procedure would be to assume that the optimal policy was to size the pipes in the network for the same number of years' load growth as single connections are sized for. This would require much less forecasting and computing than the other method; but it would not necessarily be optimal.

It is now necessary to consider the DCF appraisal of proposals to connect new customers. The bigger the amount of money which is involved and the more numerous the alternatives which are technically feasible, the more sophisticated will be the appraisal which is needed. As each major project comes up for appraisal the first step should be to investigate the alternatives to what is being proposed. In the case of each alternative, estimates are required of costs and revenues yearly during the project's life. These costs and revenues must be brought to the common denominator of present value and the risks and uncertainties of each have to be allowed for. If the best project of a set of alternatives had a present value which was positive at a discount rate of 8 per cent and if the risk attached to it was acceptable, then it would normally be authorized. However, if so many projects passed these tests that there was insufficient capital

118

to finance all of them, then more stringent criteria might have to be applied. These stages of investment appraisal are discussed in turn in the remainder of this chapter.

The Area Boards have well developed techniques for forecasting the revenue from new connections. In the case of new domestic customers the first stage is to obtain an estimate from the area sales staff of the gas appliances likely to be installed. The Area Boards know from their market research how much gas each type of appliance is likely to consume annually and from this they build up an estimate of the annual gas consumption of the proposed new customers. The annual consumption and the current price of gas are then combined to provide an estimate of the annual revenue from the project at present prices. As a check, the estimated annual revenue from the project is normally compared with the actual revenue from similar groups of existing customers. Care is taken that the proportions of local authority and private building and of houses and apartments are the same in the groups which are being compared. The time pattern of appliance installations, and hence of gas sales and revenue receipts, is assumed to level off after an initial period of build-up which may last from two to five years. The assumption that sales of gas will level off is perhaps conservative, for the evidence of recent years (but not necessarily of some periods in the more distant past) has been that as personal incomes gradually rise, standards of home comfort and hence the consumption of gas rises too. However, the Area Boards are very conscious of the dangers of over-estimating the growth of sales when making revenue forecasts. In order to safeguard themselves against any tendency on the part of local sales staff to over-estimate appliance installations, some boards do not allow these staff to consider appliances as specified unless the intent to install is backed by a signed order, a letter of intent or in the case of local authority housing estates a council minute. No doubt it is undesirable to have varying degrees of optimism in the initial figures, but unless the Area Board makes some upward adjustment to these figures at a later stage in the appraisal then the system is likely to produce conservative estimates of appliance installations and hence of sales of gas and receipts of revenue. Revenue has in fact been under-estimated in recent years, but the under-estimates were partly attributable to unexpected increases in gas consumption per appliance as well as to under-estimates of the number of appliances installed.

119

The revenue from new industrial and commercial projects is estimated along the same lines as that from new domestic projects. Consumption is estimated from detailed information about the industrial and commercial appliances to be installed and the extent to which they will be used and, together with the current industrial or commercial tariff, this provides the required estimate of annual revenue.

In principle, the costs which are relevant are those which would be incurred if, and only if, the project was authorized. However, the only costs which are forecast strictly on this basis are the immediate capital costs of connection.

If adequate pressures and flows of gas are not available from the main nearest to the proposed new customers, the engineers may have to strengthen an existing network for some distance to obtain a satisfactory supply and they may take the opportunity to reinforce part of the distribution system at the same time. In this case the immediate capital costs of the connection are the minimum capital costs which would be required if the only consideration was to provide the new customers with an adequate supply of gas. However, other categories of costs are dealt with in a different way.

The commercial departments forecast how many new customers each project will connect and how many gas appliances of each type these new customers will install. The Area Boards know from their market research how much gas each type of appliance is likely to consume both annually and on the peak day and from this they estimate the annual and peak day consumption of the new group of customers. From these data the accountants estimate the total costs of the project by multiplying by their estimates of per customer costs, per therm costs and per peak day therm costs as appropriate. In most Area Boards these multipliers are constructed in the following way.

The accountants begin by deducting from total Area Board costs all those capital costs of connection which are forecast project by project. All remaining Area Board costs are then allocated into per customer costs, per therm costs and per peak day therm costs. There is an element of arbitrariness in this allocation for some items of cost vary with more than one of the three categories. The allocation of overhead costs such as administration is particularly arbitrary; but this cannot be avoided, given the nature of the calculation. The totals of the three categories are then divided respectively by the number of the Area Board's customers and by the number of therms which the board sells annually and on the peak day. The quotients of these divisions are the three multipliers which are used to complete the cost forecasts. These multipliers are thus an approximation to part of the average accounting costs per customer, per therm and per peak day therm whereas it is marginal costs which are required.

Some boards are aware that it is marginal costs which are relevant to investment appraisal and they adapt their total cost allocations in various ways to allow for this. In the case of one board the adaptation takes the form of setting the per customer and per peak day therm costs at 25 per cent of the corresponding figures from the total cost allocation. The relationship between average and marginal costs no doubt varies to some extent from board to board. But it is hard to believe that 25 per cent of the total cost allocation in one board corresponds to the same concept as 100 per cent of it in another. The care taken to ensure that the same accounting concepts are used in all boards is not taken to ensure that all boards use the same economic concepts.

In some circumstances it is necessary to take into account the cost of conversion to natural gas. For example, if the timing of conversion is known and a large group of new customers are to be connected, there may be a case for avoiding or reducing conversion costs by providing the group with a temporary supply of natural gas from the start. There was an instance in the East Midlands Board where a temporary supply of LNG was considered as an alternative to town gas for new customers during the period preceding conversion. Similarly, in choosing routes for new high-pressure pipes it is necessary to take into account the amounts by which each alternative route would reduce the board's conversion costs. But in other cases, for example, projects to connect new housing estates, there may be no appreciable advantage in trying to take conversion into account. There will be once-for-all costs of altering appliances at the time conversion is carried out, but thereafter the cost of gas will be lower because natural gas is cheaper than town gas. The tariff will be changed to take account of both these changes in costs. Thus, the costs and revenues of a project, which spans the time of conversion will both be changed in the same direction. It is not unreasonable for the Area Boards to assume, as most of them do, that the changes will be sufficiently offsetting to be ignored in the appraisal of projects such as new housing estates.

The industry would have to change many of its established habits of thought, if it changed from its present method of costing and adopted marginal costs. For example, it would have to change its way of measuring the cost of working capital – a small, but in the present context, tell-tale item in the accounts. Since there is a lag between the time when gas is supplied and the revenue from it is received, the connection of new customers increases the amount of working capital which the Area Boards require. If the costs and revenues from connecting new customers are discounted at 8 per cent for purposes of investment appraisal, then the cost of working capital is implicitly set at 8 per cent. At the moment the Area Boards do not think of the matter in this way. They take the cost of working capital as the rate they actually pay for it – a rate lower than 8 per cent. This is appropriate for financial appraisals, but not for economic appraisals such as are under discussion.

Proposals to connect new customers are so numerous that considerable time would be required to carry out a full DCF appraisal of each one. To reduce the time spent on appraisal, all the Area Boards use short-cut methods of discounting. These short-cut methods require some simplifying assumptions, but they are perfectly adequate for many projects. Some boards confine detailed appraisal to projects which their short-cut method shows to be borderline; other boards rely on their short-cut method to determine the amount of the financial contribution which is required in any given case.

The assumption which underlies the short-cut methods of discounting used is that annual costs and revenues are constant after the end of the construction period. Capital costs include the interest cost of capital at 8 per cent during the construction period where this exceeds one year. If the revenue from the initial appliance installations is insufficient to justify a project, then the Area Boards add the revenue from the extra appliance installations which are expected to take place in the first few years of occupation. From this they decide whether to ask for a financial contribution. Sometimes they offer to forgo a financial contribution, if there is a sufficient increase in the number of gas appliances installed. They may even relax their standards somewhat if they think that to do so would create new and favourable investment opportunities which would not otherwise be open.

The following is one of the short-cut methods in use for the appraisal of new housing estates:

Let G = the gross annual revenue from the estate after the build-up period.

Let k = the proportion of this revenue which is spent on items other than estate mains and services.

Then $G(1-k)$ = the net annual revenue from the project.

Let C = the capital investment in estate mains and services.

Let n = the amortization period of capital in years.

Let r = the rate of interest per annum expressed as a decimal.

Then the estate will provide a return of r or more if:

$$G(1-k) \geqslant \frac{Cr(1+r)^n}{(1+r)^n-1} \text{ or } C \leqslant \frac{G(1-k)[(1+r)^n-1]}{r(1+r)^n}$$

The right-hand side of the second of these inequalities is then the maximum permitted capital outlay. The Area Board which used this formula considered the proportion of revenue spent on items other than estate mains and services as being stable at 90 per cent. Thus the value of k was taken as $\cdot 9$. The rate of interest had been $6\frac{1}{2}$ per cent and this value was still being taken for r although the White Paper had made it clear some time earlier that the appropriate rate was 8 per cent. Finally, n was taken as thirty years. Thus, the maximum permitted capital outlay was $1\cdot31$ G. Since there is no logical reason why the proportion of revenue expenditure on items other than estate mains and services should always be the same, a formula which allowed for variability in this ratio would be preferable. A formula which took more explicit account of load factor – a major determinant cost – is also to be preferred. In this and other respects, there is much to be said for the short-cut method used by the Scottish Board.

The planning staff of the Scottish Board have constructed a table from over 250 DCF assessments, which shows for different thermal consumptions and load factors (reflecting the different types of appliance mix), the maximum amount which can be spent per customer on mains and services to provide an 11 per cent DCF yield. Projects in which the expenditure per customer on mains and services exceeds the maximum amount given by the table are then fully appraised using an 8 per cent discount rate. It seems to us that this method is superior to that of most other boards.

Most Area Boards base their estimates of costs and revenues on unfavourable assumptions and take no separate account of risk. Another way of introducing conservatism into the estimates is to assume an unrealistically short life for each project. The Area Boards have standard accounting lives for each type of fixed asset. But the lives used in investment appraisal vary from board to board. In some boards these lives are shorter than the accounting lives and they are nowhere longer. It is difficult to see why the lives which are used for economic and accounting purposes should not be the same. Cases were noticed where the revenue from new industrial projects was assumed to continue for a shorter period than the revenue from new housing estates and the difference was explained as a way of allowing for the greater riskiness of industrial sales. Residual values too are estimated conservatively, presumably to take account of risk also.

Some Area Boards allow for risk by adding a premium to the rate used for discounting. For instance, in the appraisal of new housing estates the discount rates in use in different boards ranged between $6\frac{1}{2}$ and $12\frac{1}{2}$ per cent, the higher rates being explained as necessary to take account of risk. In some boards this same explanation was given to account for the discounting of new industrial projects at a rate higher than that used for new housing estates. In one Area Board the practice is to use a discount rate of 20 per cent for new industrial projects; in another the figure is 15 per cent.

None of the methods so far mentioned is satisfactory for the majority of projects. Where conservatism is built into the estimates at various points and in various ways the decision taker has no quantitative measure of its cumulative effect and therefore cannot know whether an appropriate allowance has been made for risk in any given case. Much the same is true if a high discount rate is used. For example, if, as some Area Boards do, allowance is made for risk by discounting at 11 per cent instead of 8 per cent, then it is relevant to ask how far the annual net revenue can fall short of the central estimate and still yield a positive present value at 8 per cent. In the case of one particular, but not necessarily typical project, which was analysed in this way, the answer was 15 per cent. But if the object was to hedge against forecasting errors of this magnitude, then it would have been better to have expressed the forecast as a range and not as a single value in the first place.

Security of supply as well as financial out-turns require analysis of risk and uncertainty. Security may be a factor from the start of a project. For example, in many cases reinforcement is prompted by the likelihood of exceeding some physical limit imposed for safety.

Security may also affect the design of a proposed project. For example, it may influence the decision whether to install a double pipeline or a single one of similar carrying capacity. Even if it arises in neither of these ways, it may still influence the final decision. For example, if a scheme was unacceptable by a small margin on a financial calculation which ignored security, it might still be accepted if it provided a significant, but unquantified, reduction in the risk of supply failure. In this case the gain in security is implicitly assigned a value not less than that sum which is required to make the project financially acceptable. It is important to state this value explicitly and to consider whether the same gain in security could not be provided in a cheaper way, if it is to be provided at all.

It is always desirable to focus attention on the origin and range of the relevant risks, if they are to be allowed for in the investment decision. One way of focusing attention on them is to make two assessments of each project, one on optimistic assumptions and the other on pessimistic assumptions. Another method is to take a single best estimate and show how it would be altered by each of a series of alternative assumptions concerning the variables which are the subject of uncertainty. These are the methods approved by the White Paper and which Area Boards should substitute for those they are using at present.

In some cases a DCF analysis will be insufficient by itself to take account of risk and uncertainty. An example is the problem of sizing the main to a new housing estate, which may be extended by further building at a later date. Assume that in one such case the adjacent land is scheduled for building and that its owner has expressed an intention to build new houses there, if he can raise sufficient capital to do so. This is quite a common situation and the Area Board's assessment of the eventual load will influence it in sizing the mains to the first houses to be built. If it sizes for future development which does not occur, then it will have put in a bigger and more costly pipe than it need have done; and if it fails to size for future development which does occur, then it will have failed to take advantage of economies of scale. The future possibilities may therefore be seen as no development, a small addition to the estate and a bigger addition. It may be supposed further that the project to connect the original estate was expected to yield 8 per cent. If the main were sized for the original estate plus the larger of the additions envisaged and if no development beyond the original estate occurred, then the present value at 8 per cent would be, say, minus £100. If the smaller of the additions was anticipated and the larger one was built then a second pipeline would have to be laid. In this case the present value at 8 per cent of the original estate plus the new development would be, say £25. The possibilities are set out in full in the following table. Given this information, for what load should the Area Board size the pipe to the original estate?

PRESENT VALUE AT 8 PER CENT OF THE ORIGINAL ESTATE
PLUS ANTICIPATED AND OTHER EXTENSIONS

	Outcomes		
Pipes to the original estate are sized on the assumption of:	*No future development*	*A small addition*	*A bigger addition*
	£	£	£
No future development	0	15	20
A small addition	−20	30	25
A bigger addition	−100	20	50

It will be assumed for simplicity that the value or utility of each outcome is proportional to its money amount.

The extreme pessimist would choose the policy, which provided as its worst outcome, a result which was preferable to the worst outcome of all other policies. In the example he would compare £0, −£20 and −£100. His solution would be not to anticipate any future development in case, by providing for a new load which did not occur, he reduced the return below its original 8 per cent. Conversely, the extreme optimist would look only at the most favourable outcomes. His solution would be to anticipate a big addition to the estate, since the best result in that case would be a surplus of £50, which would exceed the surplus of £30 or £20 which would be the most he could hope for from other policies.

Another pessimistic approach to the problem would be to choose the policy which if the worst came to the worst, would be likely to cause minimum regret. In the case of each outcome, a policy would cause regret to the extent that it provided a present value less than the maximum for that outcome. Thus, an 'indicator of regret' can be constructed in the following way. In the case of each column in the table above, the highest value is set at zero and the other present values at the amounts by which they fell below the highest present value in the column. The result is as follows:

INDICATORS OF REGRET

Pipes to the original estate are sized on the assumption of:	Outcomes		
	No future development	*A small addition*	*A bigger addition*
	£	£	£
No future development	0	15	30
A small addition	20	0	25
A bigger addition	100	10	0

The maximum regrets which the three policies would provide would be £30, £25 and £100 respectively. Therefore, on this basis the second policy (that of anticipating a small addition to the estate) would be chosen.

An alternative approach to the problem would be to try to assign probabilities to each of the outcomes envisaged. From past experience of similar cases or special features of the present case it may be possible to conclude that one outcome is slightly or considerably more probable than another. However, in order to proceed it is necessary to assign numerical values to these conclusions. Let it be supposed, for example, that the subjective assessment of the decision taker in the Area Board is that the probabilities of the three outcomes are ·1, ·4 and ·5 respectively. (The probabilities always sum to unity.) This additional information will not change the choices made by extreme optimists or pessimists, for these people are concerned solely with best and worst outcomes, irrespective of the probability that these outcomes will occur. But everyone else will want to take the probabilities into account.

Some would choose the policy which maximises the expected return. Reverting to the first table above, it will be seen that in the case of the policy which anticipates the bigger of the additions to the estate the return is $(-£100 \times ·1) + (£20 \times ·4) + (£50 \times ·5)$ or £23·0. This is higher than the expected returns from the other policies (which are £16·0 and £22·5 respectively) and therefore it would be chosen. The analysis could easily be repeated with different probabilities to show how sensitive the solution was to the particular probabilities used. When the expected return is used as the sole criterion in circumstances such as those in the example, there is a danger of big losses when unlikely but very adverse outcomes occur. A constraint may be imposed to guard against this: the Area Board might make it a rule never to accept projects which, in foreseeable but unlikely circumstances, could lead to a loss bigger than some specified amount or percentage of the initial investment.

There are other ways of choosing from among the three sizing policies; but they will not be considered here. There may also be complications. The owner of the land may express an intention to build additional houses, if and when he can raise sufficient capital to do so. In this case uncertainty relates both to the size of the eventual load and to its timing. Such cases are discussed in the technical literature on the subject and we do not consider them here.

It will have been noticed that each of the three policies was chosen by at least one of the criteria discussed. None of these criteria or of the criteria not discussed is clearly superior to all others. This is an area where there are no right and wrong methods of selection. However, the industry should find it helpful to set out its problems in a formal way and to try to express its assessments of future outcomes explicitly in terms of probability.

There is almost always more than one way of accomplishing a given objective or of using a given asset and in each case the aim is to choose the best one. At the other extreme if the investment pro-gramme is constrained by other criteria as well as the requirement to earn at least 8 per cent, then it should be clear that the projects excluded are the worst ones. Thus, where projects are mutually exclusive or resources are limited, investments should be ranked in order of merit.

Where ranking is required the practice of some Area Boards is to rank by rate of return whereas others rank by present value using a discount rate of 8 per cent. The two methods will give similar rankings in many cases and they will necessarily give similar rankings where all the investments being ranked are expected to last for the same number of years and the excess of revenue over costs does not vary from year to year. But these conditions are not always fulfilled. There is seldom a difference between the lives of alternative schemes. But the timing of costs and revenues may be uneven. Where schemes which are alternatives have time streams of net revenues which are not completely flat, the ranking may differ according to which method is used. To illustrate the difficulty simply and in a way which can easily be verified, it will be convenient to use a hypothetical example which makes no claim to realism. But the difficulty is a practical one which is encountered by the industry.

The hypothetical net revenue streams opposite provide an

	Project A			Project B			Project A minus Project B	
		Present Values			Present Values			Present Value
Year	Net Benefit	11 per cent	8 per cent	Net Benefit	12 per cent	8 per cent	Net Benefit	8 per cent
	£	£	£	£	£	£	£	£
0	−10,000	−10,000	−10,000	−9,000	−9,000	−9,000	−1,000	−1,000
1	1,110	1,000	1,028	5,599	5,000	5,185	−4,489	−4,157
2	2,464	2,000	2,111	3,764	3,000	3,226	−1,300	−1,115
3	9,576	7,000	7,603	1,404	1,000	1,115	8,172	6,488
		Zero	742		Zero	526		216

example where the ranking by present value at a discount rate of 8 per cent differs from the ranking by internal rate of return. The two projects are assumed to be alternatives and of equal and low risk.

Project *B* has a higher internal rate of return than Project *A* (12 per cent as compared with 11 per cent), but when both are discounted at 8 per cent *A* has the higher present value (£742 as compared with £526). If 8 per cent is the opportunity cost of capital to the gas industry, then the result can be taken as a demonstration that selecting the investment which is most profitable, given the terms on which additional capital is available, is not the same as maximizing the rate of return per £100 employed.

There may be lingering doubts as to whether Project *A* is sufficiently superior to Project *B* to warrant incurring the additional capital expenditure of £1,000 which is required to finance it. If the net revenues of Project *B* are subtracted from those of Project *A*, it will be seen that the expenditure of the additional £1,000 increases the present value at 8 per cent by £216. The fact that this is not negative shows that the additional capital expenditure is worth incurring.

So far it has been assumed that an unlimited supply of capital is available to finance projects which yield at least 8 per cent. This is the assumption which the Area Boards normally ought to make. However, there may be times when the amount of capital available is insufficient to finance all the projects which would yield a DCF return of 8 per cent or more. There are various ways in which the Area Boards could meet this problem. Two feasible solutions are briefly considered.

If they are to maximize present value and discount at 8 per cent all projects which are not exceptionally risky, Area Boards with limited capital will need to maximise:

$$\frac{Present\ value\ at\ 8\ per\ cent}{Capital\ costs\ arising\ during\ the\ period\ of\ capital\ scarcity}$$

Projects would be ranked by this ratio and approved in order of their ranking, highest first until the investment funds were exhausted. However, there are complications.

Let us suppose than an Area Board with a budget of £20,000 has to choose among the following projects where *A* and *B* are alternatives and so are *C* and *D* (that is, the board can choose *A* or *B* but not both, and *C* or *D* but not both).

Project	Capital cost	Present value at 8 per cent	Present value at 8 per cent / Capital Cost
	£	£	
A	10,000	742	·0742
B	9,000	526	·0584
C	3,000	150	·0500
D	11,000	495	·0450
E	7,000	70	·0100

If projects were selected by their ranking in the last column, then *A*, *C* and *E* would be chosen with a present value of £962. But *B* and *D* would be better because their present value is £1021. Thus, where projects are mutually exclusive or otherwise interdependent, the arithmetic will have to take this into account.

If investment were limited in the short run by scarcity of planning staff, such as gas engineers, or of resources, such as gas pipe of given specification, then the present value of each project at 8 per cent would be divided by manhours of gas engineers' time or yards of pipe, projects would be ranked by this ratio and the procedure would be as before. If there were constraints in more than one year of the construction period – perhaps different constraints in each year – then programming techniques might be needed to rank projects correctly.

If projects are initiated throughout a period when capital is limited and not only at the start of this period, each Area Board would have to forecast the ratios which would eliminate all but the desired amount of investment. Each board would also have to forecast how long the scarcity of capital would last. Unless these forecasts were co-ordinated in some way, or a standard figure were given by the Government, forecasts, and hence investment criteria, might vary from board to board and capital would not be efficiently allocated.

A policy which favoured projects yielding high returns when capital was scarce would mitigate the scarcity by providing big sums for reinvestment when little capital was available from other sources. Because of this it has been suggested that the discount rate should be raised to bias the investment decision in favour of quick returns. One way to introduce such a bias would be to raise the discount rate to whatever level would eliminate all but a group of projects, the total value of which was just equal to the amount of capital available to finance them. This policy would result in the use of a discount rate higher than 8 per cent and in a selection of projects different from that of the first policy considered. However, if the object of the alternative policy is to increase the returns, which are available for reinvestment during the period of temporary capital shortage, then the higher discount rate need not apply to revenue and expenditure occurring after the shortage is expected to end. It might be supposed, for example, that for the next two years insufficient capital was expected to be available to finance all projects yielding at least 8 per cent, the stringency being somewhat greater in the first year than in the second. The Government might then allow the Area Boards and other parts of the public sector to discount costs and revenues at 10 per cent if they arose in the first year, at 9 per cent if they arose in the second year and at 8 per cent if they arose in subsequent years (the figures are arbitrary and are chosen simply for illustration). As before, the figures need to be co-ordinated centrally, if forecasts and hence investment criteria are not to vary from one part of the public sector to another with consequential misallocation of resources.

12

THE MARGINAL COSTS OF COAL[1]

Marginal cost is the difference between two time streams of minimum total cost, each corresponding to a different level of demand. Since the buyer will wish to minimize his delivered costs, marginal costs need to be measured at the point where the coal is going to be used. Thus the minimum total cost which is relevant includes transport as well as production.

It is system costs which are relevant, in other words the minimum total cost of producing and transporting coal to all customers in all time periods with and without the change in demand to be costed. System costs are not necessarily local and immediate. Thus a fall in demand in a part of the country where production costs were low might not result in any changes in local production; costs might be minimized by transporting local coal further than before and closing eventually and earlier than planned a pit in a higher cost coalfield. In this case the fall in demand would give rise to no local savings in cost. But it would provide system cost savings equal to the savings at the distant pit which was closed, less the extra costs of transport which were incurred. These net system cost savings are the marginal cost of the fall in demand.

The number of marginal tons or therms to be costed will depend on the size of the order to be priced. In most cases the order will be small relative to the output of the industry and it can conveniently be assumed to be infinitely small. In this case if linear programming is used to minimize total costs, marginal cost is conveniently measured by the duals of the demand constraints.[2] But in some cases, notably those concerning supply to the electricity industry, bigger changes may have to be contemplated. If a power station is

[1] Appendix H of *Coal Prices* (*Second Report*), Report 153 of The National Board for Prices and Incomes (HMSO Cmnd. 4455, August 1970); reproduced with the permission of the Controller of Her Majesty's Stationery Office.

[2] A dual value represents the loss or gain from changing a restricting resource by one unit.

converted from coal to oil firing, the loss of sales by the coal industry is considerable, and to evaluate its marginal cost a large and permanent fall in demand would have to be costed.

The costs to the nation need to be considered in these calculations, and not the accounting costs to the NCB and the carriers. Thus, if the additional transport of coal causes congestion on the railways, the transport cost which is relevant includes the cost of the congestion, even if neither the buyers nor the sellers of coal have to pay for it. In practice, the main divergence between accounting costs and social opportunity costs arises in the case of mining labour. This is dealt with in the next chapter.

There are as many marginal costs as there are separate types of coal, centres of demand and periods of time to be considered. This makes for complexity and to explore some of the problems a study was carried out to determine the feasibility and cost of changing the output of a particular pit.

The colliery studied produces at present about 750,000 tons a year of which some 50 per cent goes to the electricity market, 30 per cent to the industrial market and 20 per cent to the domestic market. The study considered first the feasibility and cost of raising and lowering output by 250,000 tons. Plans existed to raise output to 1,000,000 tons and the cost of this increase was readily assessed. The extra eighty men who would be needed were thought to be available. A reduction to 500,000 tons required a substantial revision of the pit's plans and a reduction of about 180 jobs below the number required to produce 750,000 tons. These changes too were costed. The result established that the costs saved by reducing output by 250,000 tons exceeded the costs incurred by increasing output by 250,000 tons, indicating that marginal cost was declining in the range of output considered. The marginal cost per ton of increasing output by 250,000 tons was roughly half the average accounting cost per ton of producing 1,000,000 tons and it was far below average realizations at this particular pit. An increase to a level of annual output above 1,000,000 tons was scarcely feasible without a major reorganization, in particular without an increase in shaft capacity. Thus a major exercise would be needed to determine the marginal cost of such an increase. Such an exercise would be needed to determine whether costs could be saved by expanding output at this colliery and closing some higher cost capacity. The marginal cost of reducing output to 500,000 tons would be relevant if the NCB had to cut output and was uncertain where the cut could most advantageously be made.

The study also considered the consequences of changing the mix of output keeping the level at 750,000 tons. Such changes would require a change of machinery at the coal face, and an earlier NCB study was drawn on which examined the feasibility of using various kinds of machinery at this particular mine and the performance to be expected. Changing the types of machines would cause consequential changes in manpower requirements and these too were considered and costed. But consideration was not given to major schemes such as the substitution of skip winding for tubs, a change which might have been appropriate if most of the colliery's output was for the electricity market. The study established that the proportion of domestic coal could be increased from 20 per cent to 35 per cent, though to do so would raise the colliery's total accounting costs by some 3 per cent. Alternatively the proportion of electricity coal could be increased from 50 per cent to 65 per cent with a reduction of about $\frac{1}{2}$ per cent in total accounting costs. These results would be relevant if a decision was needed whether to specialize at this colliery more than at present in production for the electricity or domestic markets.

The study showed that at one colliery at least there was considerable flexibility in respect of the level and mix of output. However, to use such data for planning and pricing, collieries need to be considered in groups and the NCB has developed a linear programme which enables this to be done. This model was developed as an aid to Area planning. However, since it can be used to minimize the cost of meeting a specified demand subject to the constraints which the planner wishes to impose, it can also be used to determine marginal costs.

As input to the model there is required a set of production, segregation, transport, coal preparation, marketing and manpower alternatives at each pit. The production alternatives specify the seams, faces and shifts per face which can be worked and the methods of working which can be used. Information is also needed on alternative facilities for keeping the various flows of output separate, on alternatives in respect of screening, and on alternative pit to washer routes for each segregated coal flow. It is necessary to specify also the various grades and qualities which can be supplied and the coal preparation available to vary the ash and moisture content and to crush, size and blend. Manpower availability and the possibility of transferring men from one pit to another need to be specified, together with expected manpower losses from a policy of transfer. In respect of each of these sets of alternatives it is necessary to specify relevant constraints such as the capacity of the shaft and of each part of the coal preparation plant. Capacity constraints can be removed by new investment and the model can incorporate new capital projects.

If Areas could be regarded as wholly independent of one another the model would probably be adequate to determine marginal costs since it takes a great deal of detail into account. But Areas are not wholly independent since, within limits, flows from one Area can be substituted for flows from another on the initiative of either the customer or the NCB. Thus there is a need for a national model as well as an Area model. In fact the NCB have also developed a national model and it is this model which we have used to try to establish marginal costs.

The national model is a linear programme which can be used to calculate the minimum total cost of meeting demand in each of the seven selling Regions subject to constraints. The five market categories considered in the model are electricity, coke ovens, domestic bituminous, domestic naturally smokeless and other. Demand is forecast by the NCB marketing department in these five categories and in the original version of the model the total cost to be minimized is given by the sum of three items:

(a) The dependent costs of production at the collieries. These are the variable costs, incurred only if the colliery is in production. The model assumes that the cost per ton is independent of the level of production in the colliery.

(b) The costs of transporting coal from pits to market. The model assumes that the cost of transporting coal from any given Area to any sales Region is the same for all pits within the Area.

(c) The loss in proceeds through selling coal of one market type in a different market. The decline in demand for domestic coal in recent years has resulted in a surplus of large coal. The excess is crushed and sold at a lower price, mainly to the CEGB, and the loss in proceeds represents the difference between the two prices.

Apart from purely technical constraints such as, for example that costs cannot be negative, some additional limitations are imposed:

1. Certain 'banker' pits, selected by a working group set up by NCB management, are always included in the solution. These are typically pits which have development potential or which for marketing reasons the working group does not want to allow to close.
2. Demand in Scotland is satisfied only from Scottish collieries.
3. A minimum level of coking coal is maintained for certain areas.

The input to the model is the data from the NCB's national planning exercise. For this, each Area is required to submit detailed information for each pit for the years 1970–1 to 1974–5 inclusive. The information includes data on the planned output of the pit and the costs of production, with an allowance for inflation at rates set centrally by Finance Department. In addition the Areas provide 'relaxation levels' to allow for unforeseen variations in output, e.g. major stoppages at individual collieries. The sum of the colliery relaxed figures for each Area goes forward as an Area total to NCB headquarters where Area totals are themselves relaxed. There is an element of artificiality in adjusting colliery figures so that their sum equals the national relaxed total tonnage. But this is done and the model takes relaxed tonnages for each pit, adjusting the production costs accordingly, and determines which pits should produce the output needed to satisfy demand at minimum cost. Because of the relaxations, the amounts to be produced by each colliery need to be treated with caution. However, accepting this, the marginal delivered cost of each type of coal in each sales Region is given by the shadow price on the appropriate demand constraint. With five types of coal and seven sales Regions there are thirty-five shadow prices.

For the calculations which we carried out, the model and the data were modified in four ways:

1. The loss of proceeds term was removed. Since coal of a particular type is only worth what customers are willing to pay for it, there is no loss of proceeds if domestic coal which is crushed and sold in the electricity market at a reduced price could not in any case have been sold at the full domestic price. The only cost incurred by transferring the coal to the electricity market is the cost of crushing and this cost was retained in the model.
2. The constraints ensuring that only Scottish-produced coal should be consumed in Scotland were partially removed: the way in which the model was formulated made complete removal impossible in the time available. On the other hand, the other

two additional constraints in the original model, referring to banker pits and the production of coking coal, were retained as they were essentially quality constraints.

3. The allowance for general inflation was removed from the cost figures. But labour costs were inflated by 3 per cent a year or by the amount of pay increases already committed, whichever was higher. That these changes affected most pits about equally is shown by the fact that they scarcely changed the ranking of pits in order of unit production cost. Adjustments for inflation reduced unit production costs in 1974–5 by about 15 per cent for most pits, while for 1970–1 the corresponding figure was about 3 per cent.

4. Resource costs of labour were substituted for accounting costs, a matter discussed in the next chapter.

The relaxation levels employed were those originally proposed by the Areas. It was not safe to use unrelaxed values, since data are not consistently recorded between Areas. For example, in some the total output represents the amount they would like to produce while in others it represents the most they could possibly produce.

The original programme of work envisaged determination of the marginal delivered cost of each of the five types of coal in each of the seven sales Regions in each of the years 1970–1 to 1974–5. Varying by plus or minus 10 per cent the demand of each type of coal in each Region would give a range of marginal delivered costs (thus showing whether a central figure for each was robust) and it would then be necessary to work back to pit head costs by deducting transport. Pit head costs arrived at in this way would then be compared with forecast realizations and an accounting exercise would show the effect on the NCB's accounts of substituting marginal cost pricing for the present system.

The exercise should in principle take into account the changes in demand which might be expected to follow from each change in price which was contemplated. In practice it is difficult to do this for markets other than electricity. A study was planned which was designed to show the reactions of the CEGB.

The CEGB has a suite of programmes designed to minimize the delivered cost of electricity, given, among other inputs, the price of coal at groups of pits. The plan was to use these programmes jointly with the NCB's national model to reconcile demand, costs and prices in the market for electricity coal. The first step in the analysis would be to estimate what the marginal resource cost of electricity coal would be if the CEGB took the tonnages at present forecast. At prices equal to these marginal costs which were presumably not the prices on which the original forecast was based, how much coal would the CEGB want to buy? The CEGB's models could be used to answer this question. The marginal cost of the new tonnage would then have to be calculated and the cycle repeated until, by iteration, demand, costs and prices had been reconciled.

There are practical difficulties in implementing this programme of work. If the CEGB was given first choice of all the coal available, then there would be no assurance that, from the coal which was left, it would be possible to meet all non-CEGB demand. For example, so much large coal might have been crushed that domestic demand could not be satisfied. Thus, before iteration between the NCB and CEGB models could begin, there would have to be a preliminary exercise which minimized the delivered costs of meeting all demands at their points of origin. The coal not chosen for other markets in this preliminary selection would then be available to satisfy the demands of the CEGB. It would be the costs of this coal at its collieries of origin which would be used as input to the CEGB models.

13

THE RESOURCE COSTS OF MINING LABOUR[1]

Since many miners are old or live in remote areas and, in any case, have poor prospects of re-employment if they lose their jobs with the Coal Board, it appears to us that the accounting cost of mining labour overstates its cost to the nation. It may sometimes be appropriate to value resources at more or less than their accounting cost. For example, the nationalized industries are instructed to use a test discount rate of 10 per cent in appraising investment projects even though the accounting cost of new capital to them is less than 10 per cent. Thus, decisions are taken on the basis that capital costs 10 per cent and financial accounts are prepared on the basis that it costs less than 10 per cent. A similar principle could be applied to the cost of labour. This cost needs to be recorded in the accounts as the amount of money paid out in the wage bill. But, in deciding whether to increase or reduce employment it is arguable that the cost of labour should be taken as the value forgone elsewhere in the economy by retaining miners in the coal industry. This can be taken to be the highest cost which employers outside coalmining would be willing to incur to employ an ex-miner net of any social costs of the transfer. The highest cost which an employer outside coalmining would be willing to incur is in such a calculation a proxy for the marginal value product of labour, i.e. marginal physical product times marginal revenue. The suggestion is then that in taking manpower decisions the NCB should value miners' time at its social opportunity cost and not at the cost which is recorded in the accounts. This suggestion is not new.

We have undertaken preliminary studies designed to discover in what respects the industry's labour resource costs differ from accounting costs. Our approach can be illustrated by a simplified example.

[1] Appendix I of *Coal Prices (Second Report)*, Report 153 of the National Board for Prices and Incomes (HMSO Cmnd. 4455, August 1970); reproduced with the permission of the Controller of Her Majesty's Stationery Office.

The Resource Costs of Mining Labour

Assume the redundancy of 100 miners typical in respect of age, health and skill. Assume too that their redundancy may be postponed for a year and that the rate at which they are reabsorbed into local employment is independent of the date of initial redundancy. The two following time paths of re-entry into employment need to be considered.

NUMBER OF MEN RE-EMPLOYED

	Redundancies declared in year 1	Redundancies declared in year 2	Man-years of labour forgone outside coalmining by the postponement of the redundancies
By the end of year 1	50	—	50
2	80	50	30
3	100	80	20
4	100	100	—

It is clear that a result of delaying redundancies for a year is to forgo a stream of output in industries other than mining: the output from 50 men in year 1, 30 in year 2 and 20 in year 3. It will be noted that the undiscounted sum of these values equals 100. This must be the case if (i) the re-employment rate is independent of the date of redundancy, and (ii) re-employment eventually rises to 100 (i.e. no ex-miner dies or retires before he is re-employed). More generally, if (i) holds, the undiscounted sum of differences will equal the eventual re-employment level, whatever this happens to be. If (i) and (ii) hold, the only factor making the resource cost of labour lower than its accounting cost is the application of a discount rate to bring outputs forgone to a present value. There is scope for argument as to what rate of discount would be appropriate in this context. In fact the test discount rate of 10 per cent was used.

In the example it is convenient to use man-years of labour forgone outside coalmining as an index of output forgone. Thus with a 10 per cent discount rate the stream of outputs forgone would be as follows:

	Output forgone outside coalmining by the postponement of mining redundancies	Present value discounted at 10 per cent
By the end of year 1	50	45·5
2	30	24·8
3	20	15·0
		85·3

The present value of 85·3 can be related to a value in the original job of 100 discounted for a year (since it has been assumed that all sums are payable at the end of the year). Thus in this example, the average resource cost per man is 93·8 per cent of average wages plus wages charges in the coal mine.[2] The analysis can be applied to any period during which redundancies may be delayed; and it can be applied where re-employment rates vary with the date of initial redundancy. Thus it has considerable generality, though the numerical answers are only as good as the data and assumptions on which they are based.

The difficulties concerning the data and assumptions can be illustrated by considering to what extent and with what delay labour costs and unemployment are affected by mining redundancies.

Although in calculating resource costs it is the cost to the employer which is relevant and not the reward to the employee, as a first approximation the two can be assumed to be correlated so closely that estimation can start from the highest earnings outside coalmining which an ex-miner could expect. A convenient starting point would be the actual earnings of ex-miners who have had to transfer to other industries, but no such information is available at present. Another approach would be to assume that the earnings of ex-miners would be the average earnings outside coalmining in the part of the country or commuter area where they live. This would probably be an overstatement, partly because many ex-miners are old and past their earnings peak (their earnings may be below the average for the coal industry), and partly because many of the most highly paid occupations would in any case be closed to them.

The social costs of transfer are probably very variable and they would need to be quantified case by case. They might raise or lower the social opportunity costs of ex-miners; but they are likely to be significant only where a relatively young pit labour force is affected, and where the relationships between the supply and demand of particular types of social capital vary widely between the places of migrants' origin and destination.

In places where miners' opportunity costs are below their accounting costs and expected to remain so, a new recruit may have an opportunity cost above his accounting wage even if the NCB has to compete with other industries for his services and pay a wage no

[2] $\dfrac{85\cdot3}{100 \times \cdot909} \times 100 = 93\cdot8.$

lower than other industries offer. This will apply if early commitment to the coalmining industry reduces the earnings potential of the new recruit in later life. In principle, the present worth of any such reduction should be added as a premium to the accounting wage to arrive at the resource cost of a new recruit.

In practice it was assumed in our calculations that employers outside coalmining would be willing to pay as much as the NCB for miner's time.

As a stage in the estimation of resource costs it is necessary to estimate the probable increase in unemployment which could follow from particular decisions by the NCB. In respect of a particular pit, for example, the decision might be whether to close down, contract output, substitute machinery for men or continue present levels and methods of working.

In order to estimate the relevant increase in unemployment, a comparison needs to be made between two time streams of entry into unemployment and exit from it. The relevant comparison might be thought to be between a time stream including mining redundancies and one excluding them. But all pits must close sooner or later if only because of the exhaustion of coal reserves. Therefore the comparison needs to be between redundancies occurring at one period and at another. For example, the decision might be whether to defer a colliery closure for a year. But the relevant interval could be longer. An extreme case is that in which mining redundancies might be postponed for up to thirty years by a decision to install a new coal-fired power station instead of a nuclear one.

The simplest situation to analyse is one in which Government policy causes shifts in the local demand for labour which exactly match shifts in supply. In these circumstances local unemployment would remain constant *ex hypothesi* and there would be no problem. The relevance of this is that given sufficient foreknowledge the Government could hope to offset the rundown of mining manpower by creating new work in the regions. If complete success is assumed for regional policy by, say, 1980, then mining decisions should not be influenced by the possibility of causing local unemployment after that date. For the interim period the assumption might be made that the present imbalance in regional job prospects would lessen but not necessarily at an even rate. For instance a slow improvement might be expected during the first half of the 1970s and a faster improvement in the second half. In any case, the assumption might be made that the longer redundancies were deferred, the less unemployment they would create. This needs to be qualified to the extent that the time interval between successive redundancies is also important: the more ex-miners there are among those already unemployed in any commuter area, the more unemployment in that area new mining redundancies are likely to cause (because the characteristics of those newly unemployed will more nearly match those of people already unemployed). In any case the principle is clear that, in general, resource costs should be assumed to rise towards the level of accounting costs, though perhaps at different rates in different periods and parts of the country.

An alternative and equally extreme assumption is that the Government will be completely unsuccessful in accelerating the rate of new job creation in the regions. In these circumstances an increase in the supply of labour resulting from mining redundancies might lower local wages (or slow their rise) and this could be expected to cause some increases in the local demand for labour. The additional availability of labour might also cause some vacancies to be filled which would otherwise have remained unfilled. But the net effect would be that unemployment would rise, and, depending on the macro-economic policies being pursued by the Government, there might also be multiplier effects to be taken into account which would raise unemployment further.

It is commonly alleged that expectations of a faster decline in coalmining would be self-fulfilling since they would cause morale to weaken and this in turn would cause the growth of productivity to slow. Coal would then become less competitive with other fuels and sales would fall. It is not clear that miners are mainly influenced by the prospects for the industry, as distinct from the prospects for the particular pit where they work. But some may be. For example, new recruitment might become more difficult if, as is likely, potential entrants were better informed about national prospects than about the prospect for the local pit; and potential colliery managers, a group who can expect to move from pit to pit during a successful career, may put less effort into their work as closures reduce their promotion prospects. It is difficult to evaluate such arguments and they deserve to be subjected to systematic research.

It will be clear from this discussion that a great many assumptions must underlie any estimate of the unemployment which would be likely to follow from particular decisions by the NCB. Against this background we now turn to the estimates of unemployment from which our estimates of resource costs were built up.

A way of estimating future unemployment has been suggested by Haveman and Krutilla.[3] They start from the proposition that a newly redundant person may himself become unemployed, or, by taking a job which someone else would have taken, he may be responsible indirectly for initiating or prolonging that other person's unemployment. The higher the local level of unemployment, the higher will be the probability that a newly redundant person will add directly or indirectly to the numbers unemployed. Following Haveman and Krutilla's approach, it might be assumed that if local unemployment was below, say, $1\frac{1}{2}$ per cent (a figure chosen to represent a minimum frictional level) then all newly redundant miners would be re-employed immediately and without causing any unemployment indirectly; and if local unemployment was above, say, 20 per cent, no newly redundant miner could expect to be re-employed at all. These assumptions establish two points on a curve which then has to be drawn in some credible fashion. In fact, Haveman and Krutilla use a sine curve and establish upper and lower bounds as well as best estimates.

We have experimented with a simple model of the kind used by Haveman and Krutilla. Given a forecast of the relationships between regional and national unemployment percentages, region by region and year by year, the model is required to predict re-employment rates, i.e. the proportion of those made redundant in each region who will be re-employed a year later, net of indirect increases in unemployment. It was assumed that where the regional unemployment percentage was below or equal to the national average, the re-employment rate would be 100 per cent, i.e. all newly redundant miners would be re-employed within a year and there would, by the end of the year, be no indirect increase in unemployment. At the other extreme when regional unemployment was $2\frac{1}{2}$ or more times the national average the re-employment rate would be 30 per cent, a figure chosen to represent induced migration. Between these limits the relationship between regional unemployment relatives and regional re-employment rates was assumed to be linear.

Such simple models lack empirical content and fail to use all the

---

[3] *Unemployment, idle capacity and the evaluation of public expenditure*, by Robert H. Haveman and John V. Krutilla (Resources for the Future, The Johns Hopkins Press, 1968.)

data which are available. Therefore an additional approach was adopted, based on NCB data about the ages of redundant miners together with survey information on the duration of their unemployment. This alternative approach took into account only the unemployment and re-employment of ex-miners. Thus, indirect, multiplier and migration effects of mining redundancies were excluded from the calculations.

Ex-miners over 55 were reabsorbed into employment more slowly than younger men even before the miners' redundancy payments scheme was introduced in 1967, and an effect of the scheme has been to exaggerate this difference. Therefore it is necessary to consider men over 55 separately from the rest.

The men made redundant by a pit closure may not be the men employed at the closing pit: the NCB may encourage older men at neighbouring pits to volunteer for redundancy so that younger men from the closing pit can be transferred. The scope for transfer depends on a number of factors which vary from one case to another, the rate of manpower rundown in the relevant commuter area being an important one. The more rapid the rate or manpower rundown, the more closely will the age distribution of the men made redundant resemble the age distribution at the closing pit. Therefore, in respect of each future colliery closure two assumptions have been made as to the split between the over 55s and the rest, corresponding respectively to national rates of manpower rundown in the region of 7 and 12 per cent. These assumptions in turn imply a pattern of regional rates of rundown corresponding to each national rate.

Initially, those 55 and over and those under 55 are treated separately in the calculations. In both cases estimates are made for groups of pits of the average percentage of redundant miners who would be re-employed in each of the 3 years after closure. The output foregone by maintaining a pit in production from, for example, 1970 to 1971 is calculated as the sum of the discounted first order differences of the re-employment percentages for years 1, 2 and 3 after closure in 1970 and for years 1 and 2 after closure in 1971. This follows the procedure of the simplified example. (It is assumed that there are no differences in the alternative output streams 3 years after a pit closure has been delayed for one year; calculated differences are thought to be within the margin of error of the calculations.) The calculations are repeated for closure delays of one year in 1971, 1972,

1973, 1974 and 1975; and by summing the present value of single year delays, resource costs are derived for multi-year delays.

If the industry's rate of contraction is given, then resource costs should indicate in which parts of the country the contraction could most advantageously be concentrated. However, if the rate of contraction is itself to be determined, then resource costs have a wider application.

INDEX